LONGMAN CRITICAL ES

OThELLO

William Shakespeare

Editors:
Linda Cookson
Bryan Loughrey

Longman Critical Essays

Editors: Linda Cookson and Bryan Loughrey

Titles in the series:

Antony and Cleopatra   0 582 06051 6
Emma   0 582 00653 8
The General Prologue to the Canterbury Tales   0 582 03790 5
Hamlet   0 582 00648 1
Julius Caesar   0 582 07579 3
Keats   0 582 00652 X
Philip Larkin   0 582 03810 3
King Lear   0 582 00649 X
Macbeth   0 582 00650 3
Measure for Measure   0 582 07576 9
The Merchant of Venice   0 582 07575 0
The Metaphysical Poets   0 582 06048 6
A Midsummer Night's Dream   0 582 07580 7
Much Ado About Nothing   0 582 03791 3
Othello   0 582 07578 5
The Pardoner's Prologue and Tale   0 582 06049 4
Richard II   0 582 03792 1
Romeo and Juliet   0 582 07577 7
The Tempest   0 582 00651 1
Twelfth Night   0 582 06050 8
The Waste Land   0 582 00655 4
Wuthering Heights   0 582 00654 6

CONTENTS

Preface   **5**

Introduction: How to use this volume   **7**

Essays   **9**

The Lodovico Report
Mark Spencer Ellis   9

Tragedy or satire?
Graham Holderness   23

The semiotics of *Othello*
Cedric Watts   33

'Silence that dreadful bell':
Othello and critical neurosis
Brean Hammond   43

'When you shall these unlucky deeds relate':
Othello and story-telling
Mark Thornton Burnett   61

Why Othello was right to choose Cassio
Angus Alton   73

One that loved too well:
a positive view of Othello's love
Peter Cairns   84

The Willow scene
Claire Saunders   96

Unholy alliance: Othello and Iago
Ronald Draper   106

'Look well to their linen'
Neil Taylor   119

A practical guide to essay writing   **129**

Introduction   129

How to plan an essay   130

Style sheet   141

Suggestions for further reading   **147**

PREFACE

Like all professional groups, literary critics have developed their own specialised language. This is not necessarily a bad thing. Sometimes complex concepts can only be described in a terminology far removed from everyday speech. Academic jargon, however, creates an unnecessary barrier between the critic and the intelligent but less practised reader.

This danger is particularly acute where scholarly books and articles are re-packaged for a student audience. Critical anthologies, for example, often contain extracts from longer studies originally written for specialists. Deprived of their original context, these passages can puzzle and at times mislead. The essays in this volume, however, are all specially commissioned, self-contained works, written with the needs of students firmly in mind.

This is not to say that the contributors — all experienced critics and teachers — have in any way attempted to simplify the complexity of the issues with which they deal. On the contrary, they explore the central problems of the text from a variety of critical perspectives, reaching conclusions which are challenging and at times mutually contradictory.

They try, however, to present their arguments in a direct, accessible language and to work within the limitations of scope and length which students inevitably face. For this reason, essays are generally rather briefer than is the practice; they address quite specific topics; and, in line with examination requirements, they incorporate precise textual detail into the body of the discussion.

They offer, therefore, working examples of the kind of essay-writing skills which students themselves are expected to develop. Their diversity, however, should act as a reminder that in the field of literary studies there is no such thing as a 'model' answer. Good essays are the outcome of a creative engagement with literature, of sensitive, attentive reading and careful thought. We hope that those contained in this volume will encourage students to return to the most important starting point of all, the text itself, with renewed excitement and the determination to explore more fully their own critical responses.

How to use this volume

Obviously enough, you should start by reading the text in question. The one assumption that all the contributors make is that you are already familiar with this. It would be helpful, of course, to have read further — perhaps other works by the same author or by influential contemporaries. But we don't assume that you have yet had the opportunity to do this and any references to historical background or to other works of literature are explained.

You should, perhaps, have a few things to hand. It is always a good idea to keep a copy of the text nearby when reading critical studies. You will almost certainly want to consult it when checking the context of quotations or pausing to consider the validity of the critic's interpretation. You should also try to have access to a good dictionary, and ideally a copy of a dictionary of literary terms as well. The contributors have tried to avoid jargon and to express themselves clearly and directly. But inevitably there will be occasional words or phrases with which you are unfamiliar. Finally, we would encourage you to make notes, summarising not just the argument of each essay but also your own responses to what you have read. So keep a pencil and notebook at the ready.

Suitably equipped, the best thing to do is simply begin with whichever topic most interests you. We have deliberately organised each volume so that the essays may be read in any order. One consequence of this is that, for the sake of clarity and self-containment, there is occasionally a degree of overlap between essays. But at least you are not forced to follow one — fairly arbitrary — reading sequence.

Each essay is followed by brief 'Afterthoughts', designed to highlight points of critical interest. But remember, these are only there to remind you that it is *your* responsibility to question what you read. The essays printed here are not a series of 'model' answers to be slavishly imitated and in no way should they be regarded as anything other than a guide or stimulus for your own thinking. We hope for a critically involved response: 'That was interesting. But if *I* were tackling the topic . . . !'

Read the essays in this spirit and you'll pick up many of the skills of critical composition in the process. We have, however, tried to provide more explicit advice in 'A practical guide to essay writing'. You may find this helpful, but do not imagine it offers any magic formulas. The quality of your essays ultimately depends on the quality of your engagement with literary texts. We hope this volume spurs you on to read these with greater understanding and to explore your responses in greater depth.

A note on the text

Unless otherwise indicated, all references are to the New Penguin Shakespeare edition of *Othello*, ed. Kenneth Muir.

Mark Spencer Ellis

Mark Spencer Ellis is Head of English at Forest School, and a Chief Examiner in English A level for the London Schools Examinations Board.

ESSAY

The Lodovico Report

Lodovico, the representative of the Venetian state, has the final words in *Othello*. There is nothing odd in this; most Shakespearean tragedies end with the highest ranking figure delivering a judgement on what has happened. *King Lear*, both with the confusion as to whether Albany or Edgar should be credited with the last speech, and with that speech's acknowledgement of the inadequacy of 'official' words to do justice to what has passed — 'Speak what we feel, not what we ought to say' (*King Lear*, V.3.323) — is unique. Otherwise it is the winners, Fortinbras (*Hamlet*), Malcolm (*Macbeth*), or Caesar (*Antony and Cleopatra*), who point us to a new age and sum up the dead in terms which suit their own hopes for the future. Fortinbras eulogises Hamlet as a great potential military leader, shrewdly hijacking the ineffective dead prince's popularity and redefining him as having qualities which he, Fortinbras, possesses. It is necessary for Malcolm to paint Macbeth and Lady Macbeth in the most sweeping and black terms in order to direct his subjects to the new world his reign promises. We accept these final speeches as political necessities but we hardly acquiesce in the judgements. Hamlet would probably have been a rotten military leader, and there is not much left in either *Macbeth* or *Antony and Cleopatra* if we really think that Macbeth was just a 'butcher', his wife 'fiend-like', or that Antony and Cleopatra's essence was in their being 'a pair so famous'.

In all these examples there is a perceived gap between the final judgement and the way the audience actually responds. The winners have to redefine the dead in order to shape the future. That redefinition is concerned with the political necessities of guaranteeing that the speaker's values are the ones carried on in the future. *Othello* is odd. Most performances encourage us to believe that Lodovico is reflecting exactly what we will think. There is no gap. It was all a great pity, it was all Iago's fault, Iago isn't really a human being.

The speech is enormously comforting. The opening lines place Iago beyond the norms of humanity. As a 'Spartan dog' (V.2.357) he is particularly unfeeling. He is not 'as fell' but 'more fell' (line 358) than the pangs of anguish or of hunger, and more so than the force which dominates the imagery in the play, the sea. When our newspapers label particularly horrific criminals as 'monsters' or 'animals' the function of these words is to comfort the readers; they reassure us that people who are responsible for such actions are not really like us, cannot be thought of as part of the human race. 'The tragic loading of this bed' (line 359), the three bodies, are all exclusively Iago's responsibility: 'This is thy work' (line 360). Othello's 'fortunes' (line 362) assume a momentum of their own in that Gratiano is told 'they succeed on you' (line 363). There is no disquieting pause when material possessions seem ownerless. Cassio is then urged to spare no tortures in breaking Iago's body and revealing him as 'hellish' (line 364) rather than human. 'O, enforce it!' (line 365) is the bitter revenge of the outraged state. And it is to this 'state' (line 366) that Lodovico will deliver his report. He will 'relate' 'this heavy act' (line 367). Note the terms used. 'Relate' implies that simple linear narrative is all that is needed. It was all very unfortunate. This is what happened. It was all Iago's fault. (There's nothing concerning its values and attitudes about which the Venetian state needs to examine itself.)

It is with the unspoken bracketed conclusion that the official whitewash will be most concerned. It is essential to the political stability of Venice that the Senate does not make mistakes. If things go wrong it is because individuals are wicked (Iago) or have become unstable (Othello). Lodovico's immediate response when Othello strikes Desdemona is most revealing:

My lord, this would not be believed in Venice,
Though I should swear I saw't.

(IV.1.242–243)

For Venice to believe would mean that Venice had slipped up in its assessment of Othello. Lodovico is desperate for an explanation which will keep intact the Senate's reputation for making wise appointments:

Is this the noble Moor, whom our full senate
Call all-in-all sufficient? Is this the nature
Whom passion could not shake? Whose solid virtue
The shot of accident nor dart of chance
Could neither graze nor pierce?

(IV.1.266–270)

This speech is not so much to do with Othello as with the Senate's credibility, and, characteristically, it is Iago who knows what answer is required: 'He is much changed' (line 271). If Othello has gone mad, then it is possible to assert that it was a correct judgement to call him 'all-in-all sufficient'. 'Are his wits safe? Is he not light of brain?' (line 272) anxiously enquires Lodovico in the next line, and his final remark in the scene, 'I am sorry that I am deceived in him' (line 284) expresses his relief that Othello really is different from when he was in Venice.

There are two productions of *Othello*, available on video, which will almost certainly be regarded as those to be watched and analysed by students of the play. The first is the 1964 production by John Dexter, starring Laurence Olivier, Maggie Smith and Frank Finlay as Othello, Desdemona and Iago respectively. The second has Willard White, Imogen Stubbs and Ian McKellen in the leading roles, and was directed by Trevor Nunn in 1989 and first broadcast in June 1990. Each is dominated by an individual performance, those of Olivier and McKellen, but in order to clarify this essay's argument I shall refer to them as the Dexter and Nunn productions because it is in the cuts and the choice of emphasis that the overall thrust of each takes its individuality.

The first area where both of these productions edge the audience firmly towards a judgement of the play which uses the terms of the Lodovico Report, concentrating on individual character and ignoring political imperatives, is in the handling of Act I scene 3. Even though the sense of personal feeling is stressed in the run-up to this scene, the sources of real power have also been clearly set out. Brabantio's immediate response to being raised is to assert himself in terms of his political status and power:

> My spirit and my place have in them power
> To make this bitter to thee.
>
> (I.1.105–106)

It is not sympathy for which he will appeal in his hunt for Desdemona and Othello; his authority will provide what is needed:

> At every house I'll call —
> I may command at most.
>
> (I.1.181–182)

Iago recognises that Othello's security depends not on 'guilt' or 'innocence' but on his importance to the state in this specific political crisis:

> For I do know the state,
> However this may gall him with some check,
> Cannot with safety cast him; for he's embarked
> With such loud reason to the Cyprus wars,
> Which even now stand in act, that for their souls
> Another of his fathom they have none
> To lead their business.
>
> (I.1.148–154)

Othello's safety is solely based on the vital function he performs. These clear standards are laid down at the beginning of the play, and immediately serve to undermine Othello's belief that it is his merits which will defend him. His remarks to Iago at the beginning of I.2 reveal an uneasy awareness of what is, and of what he would like to be the case. In answering his Ancient's warning that Brabantio 'hath in his effect a voice potential/ As double as the Duke's' (lines 13–14), he tries to reduce Brabantio's force to the intensely personal motive of 'spite' (line 17). He then counters Iago's warnings by acknowledging his own reliance on his usefulness:

> My services, which I have done the signory,
> Shall out-tongue his complaints.
>
> (lines 18–19)

The wording carefully distances himself from his function. Othello's self-image is that of an individual with certain innate qualities. He performed these 'services' but they do not constitute him. His ancestry, 'I fetch my life and being/ From men of royal siege' (lines 21–22) are what he *is*, the services are what he *does*. However, in the same scene he shows an unconscious awareness of how he is defined when languidly teasing the indignant Brabantio. Having asserted himself over the potential brawl — 'Hold your hands,/ Both you of my inclining and the rest' (lines 80–81) — he poses what seems to be a disinterested question to the Senator: 'Where will you that I go/ To answer this your charge?' (lines 84–85). The trap depends on his knowing where he has to go, irrespective of Brabantio's wishes ('To prison'), and what follows is public humiliation for the older man:

> What if I do obey?
> How may the Duke be therewith satisfied,
> Whose messengers are here about my side,
> Upon some present business of the state
> To bring me to him?
>
> (lines 87–91)

Brabantio's shocked silence and expression of wounded pride are clearly pointed in that it is the Officer who speaks next, and feels obliged to reassure Brabantio that his status and power have not been totally undermined:

> 'Tis true, most worthy signor:
> The Duke's in council, and your noble self
> I am sure is sent for.
>
> (lines 91–93)

However, the way in which *Othello* is normally played suggests that these essentially political forces are only minor, providing a 'background' against which the personal drama and tragedy can be played out. The Programme Notes to the Nunn production are emphatic in their dismissal of anything other than 'emotional concentration' as the centre of the play:

> Every aspect of the play seems designed for emotional concentration. In the other great tragedies, one element of their greatness is the way in which a specific moment in human time and place expands to encompass a vast surrounding universe or society. But in *Othello* there is no other world such as that which the ghosts in *Hamlet* and *Julius Caesar* or the Witches in *Macbeth* draw into those plays; there is no impinging society like that which virtually causes the deaths of Romeo and Juliet; and there is no significant connection made between the personal erotic tempest and the great world such as we find in *Antony and Cleopatra*.[1]

This is a view which acquiesces in Othello's self-image. True, it allows for disagreement. Othello may be mistaken in suggesting that he is 'not easily jealous' (V.2.341) but a 'correct' view would be that the root of the tragedy lies in his being wrong about that. This is an approach which excludes all impulses which cannot be defined within the concept of the play being a drama of character, of personality — in short, a 'domestic' tragedy.

In fact I.3 opens with forty-six lines which stress the forces which provide the dramatic impulse. Venice is facing a crisis. A city state, built on that most unstable and threatening of elements, the water, is threatened with an invasion of a colony. Turkey is not simply a large and hostile power but is also much closer in geographical terms to Cyprus than Venice is. What is more, it is representative of an entirely different culture. The Duke and Senators are considering their response to the potential invasion. Certainty is their first priority; is the Turkish fleet of 'a hundred and seven galleys' (line 3), 'a hundred and forty' (line 4), or 'two hundred' (line 4)? The First Senator draws on his experience to predict that aiming for Rhodes is 'a pageant/ To keep us in false gaze' (lines 18–19), and he enjoys his moment of self-congratulation when anticipating the Turks' movements having joined with an after fleet: 'Ay, so I thought. How many, as you guess?' (line 36). At line 47 the 'domestic' cast enters, but

---

[1] Norman Sanders, Programme Notes for the 1989 Royal Shakespeare Company *Othello* at The Other Place and The Young Vic.

the emphasis in the Duke's greeting is entirely on the need for Othello to sail for Cyprus. Indeed, his words to Brabantio:

> I did not see you: welcome gentle signor;
> We lacked your counsel and your help tonight.

(lines 50–51)

seem to be prompted first by his not having noticed Brabantio in his eagerness to give Othello his commission, and secondly by Brabantio's expression of injured self-importance.

Politeness requires that the Duke listens to Brabantio's complaints, but when these complaints cast doubt on the political necessities which overrule his grievances, the Duke's responses are unambiguous. The outraged parent cites:

> . . . this Moor, whom now it seems
> Your special mandate for the state affairs
> Hath hither brought.

(lines 71–73)

Brabantio does not want to acknowledge that he is outgunned; 'seems' is a plea to be reassured that this is not the case. However, the Duke prompts Othello to provide an explanation for this. To read his question as an accusation is to ignore the prevailing realities. 'What in your part can you say to this?' (line 74) is asking Othello to solve the problem. It is as if the War Cabinet had been threatened in its preparation of the Falklands Task Force by the domestic difficulties of the Commander-in-Chief. It is inconceivable that business would seriously be suspended while these matters were debated. Politeness requires a pause to listen to the problems, but the invasion requires an immediate solution to them.

The pointers to the seriousness with which this particular War Cabinet takes Brabantio's complaint can be seen in the conclusion to the questioning of Othello and Desdemona. First the Duke 'comforts' Brabantio with a series of inappropriate proverbs (lines 200–207), made the more artificial by the self-conscious rhyming as if addressed to a child. Brabantio responds with sarcasm:

> So let the Turk of Cyprus us beguile,
> We lose it not so long as we can smile

(lines 208–209)

But his bitterness undermines itself. The point which he has not grasped is that the Duke does not acknowledge the importance of the marriage when compared with the political and military crisis. Othello's function overrides all other considerations about his behaviour. This artificiality serves to foreground the business-like prose with which the Duke gets down in line 219 to the central concerns of the meeting. The second indication of the extent to which the marriage has merited serious consideration is seen in the Duke's proposal about where Desdemona should lodge while Othello is in Cyprus: 'If you please,/ Be't at her father's' (lines 237–238). This must rank as one of the least popular suggestions in the whole of English literature, uniting as it does Brabantio, Othello and Desdemona, none of whom countenance it for a second. He could not possibly have said this had he been seriously concerned with the issue. The implication is simple: 'sort it out between yourselves at once but do not bother me about it'. Just in case this point had not been grasped, the Duke indicates his impatience with the whole business as he gives Othello his final orders:

> Be it as you shall privately determine,
> Either for her stay, or going. Th'affair cries haste,
> And speed must answer it. You must hence tonight.
>
> (lines 272–274)

Although they differ in emphasis, both of the productions under consideration reduce the threat to Cyprus to the level of disposable background. Dexter's Duke, Harry Lomax, invites Othello to take centre stage with an encouraging 'Say it, Othello' (line 126) which suggests that he would much rather hear about the wooing of Desdemona than organise a task force. Indeed, he nods in approving wonder at the mention of 'Anthropophagi' (line 143). The overall effect is to reduce the Head of State to an absurd figure whose 'Be't at her father's' suggests that even after giving them his full attention he still did not understand the feelings of the three people whose emotions had just been laid out for his inspection. As this production also cuts the first 48 lines of the scene, we are left with an impression of an Othello totally capable of deciding the course of his own life through a combination of nobility, charm and emotion.

The Nunn production does suggest the air of an emergency

Cabinet meeting but the effect of Willard White standing to address a seated Duke and Senators is still to imply that the war can be suspended while the emotional crisis is sorted out. The suggestion that Desdemona should stay with her father is as peculiarly fatuous as in the production twenty-five years earlier. The Programme Notes, quoted earlier, make the standpoint clear:

> Of course, Venice in all its political and commercial importance is the seed bed of the main action and the early scenes do contain some discussion of the Christian wars against the Turks; but even in the first act Senate scene the dramatic emphasis is on Othello's marriage, and the military expedition to Cyprus is important only for its dramatic function in isolating Desdemona from her normal surroundings.

The terms in which the characters see themselves in this scene are never challenged or questioned throughout either production. And their conclusions do nothing to suggest that we should look beyond Othello's agonised final question of Iago:

> Will you, I pray, demand that demi-devil
> Why he hath thus ensnared my soul and body?
>
> (V.2.298–299)

Dexter ignores the brisk presence of the officers to the extent of allowing Othello a free shot at a kneeling Iago at line 284. Othello's grief dominates, and, in an unusual reading of Lodovico's final speech, 'The object poisons sight:/ Let it be hid' (lines 360–361) is a furious reference to Iago who is carried off with a moan of pain calculated to appeal to an audience looking forward to the prospect of his being tortured.

The final haunting image of Nunn's production is of Iago, patently responsible for the 'tragic loading of the bed', gazing at his work with an impenetrable and enigmatic expression: wonder, satisfaction, love? We don't know. But it is an invitation to speculate, and to ponder on why Iago did it. 'This is thy work' is an accusatory bellow, followed by a cut which leads the text straight on to the request for particularly violent 'censure' of the villain.

What, then, is the matter with Lodovico's 'explanation' of what happened? We may, from the distance of 300 years, laugh at Thomas Rymer's (ironic) view that *Othello* illustrates that ladies should 'look well to their linen', but do the mesmerising individual performances in the Nunn production amount to a more profound moral than that, on a foreign posting, one should avoid having a criminal psychopath as one's personal standard-bearer? The limits of this sort of approach are precisely that it demands a series of character sketches as a response which is designed to prompt us into 'understanding' the figures who have appeared in the drama.

Iago's final words are an excellent illustration of how such a reading closes down our field of enquiry. In answer to Othello's bewildered question, he says:

> Demand me nothing; what you know, you know:
> From this time forth I never will speak word.

> (V.2.300–301)

In concentrating on the second line as the preservation of an enigma, a refusal to explain himself, productions reduce the actual answer to the question to a meaningless statement of limitations. But 'what you know, you know' is also the only possible answer. It is all there, on the surface, in Iago's actions. No further illumination can be gained from looking closer. Just observe what Iago does, and you will 'understand' him to the fullest extent that understanding can reach.

To analyse Iago in terms of motivation, conscious or unconscious, is to be condemned to a nightmare of fruitless speculation. Just when a monologue seems to reveal his deepest feelings:

> And nothing can, or shall, content my soul
> Till I am evened with him, wife for wife

> (II.1.289–290)

we find the next line showing that he prepared to contemplate alternatives, 'Or failing so', just when he stated a non-negotiable absolute. He sees events in intensely personal terms, casting himself as a spider (II.1.165–166), and as a manipulative devil in his gloating monologue in II.3.326–352. It is 'my poison' (III.3.322) which is working on Othello, and 'my medicine' (IV.1.45) which reduces the General to an epileptic wreck. This self-definition is one which is thoroughly endorsed at the end of the play when the other characters refer to Iago as 'precious villain', 'notorious villain', 'that same villain', 'damnèd slave', 'viper', 'villain', 'wretch', 'demi-devil', 'villain', 'most heathenish and most gross', 'damnèd villain', 'pernicious caitiff' and 'slave' all within the space of 100 lines. Iago has triumphed; he is seen as he would like to see himself.

But there is not really much evidence to suggest that we have been watching evil incarnate. Iago operates more like a Judo contestant than a puppeteer; it is the momentum of his victims which he utilises. What he has is an instinct for the jugular. Roderigo is obsessed with Desdemona, so Iago holds out the prospect of bedding her. Cassio is desperate for reinstatement as Lieutenant; this is what Iago offers. Lodovico, as we have seen, wants to be reassured that Othello has changed; Iago provides that reassurance. Othello demands certainty, and Iago provides it. It is stimulation rather than motivation which prompts Iago's behaviour. 'Pleasure and action make the hours seem short' (II.3.368), he proclaims. Pleasure and action are synonymous in his world, as are 'sport and profit' (I.3.380). Iago exposes the terrifying social insecurities of Venetian society but is himself unaware of any forces which lie beyond the world of impulse, will and response.

A serious examination of what constitutes the tragedy in *Othello* has to examine these shaping forces. There are hardly any moments in the play when the characters themselves come at all close to recognising them. Othello's:

> Yet 'tis the plague of great ones;
> Prerogatived are they less than the base.
> 'Tis destiny unshunnable, like death

(III.3.270–272)

is not a serious look at the limits of individual willpower. It is simply an anguished howl of self-pity. What is shocking about his final speech is not so much his extraordinary lack of self-knowledge in categorising himself as 'not easily jealous' (V.2.341) but that he embraces those values which have destroyed him, the strict hierarchy of Venice which values him strictly as an outstanding military commander. 'Othello's occupation's gone' (III.3.354) is spoken as a reflection on his sense of security, but the statement has been just as true from the moment in II.1 when the Third Gentleman announces that Othello has become redundant: 'Our wars are done' (line 20). It is in Venetian terms that he defines himself at the end; he is resigning his membership of a white Christian civilisation. His naïvety reduces him to the level of 'the base Indian' (V.2.343), and the words immediately before he stabs himself are horrific in the way he presents himself as the lowest form of being, a non-Christian who 'traduced the state' (line 350). 'A malignant and a turbaned Turk' (line 349) has the force of an axiom. One cannot imagine a benevolent and a turbaned Turk. And yet this assumption echoes the words used of him at the beginning of the play. 'The gross clasps of a lascivious Moor' (I.1.127) does not allow for the possibility of there being Moors who aren't too interested in sex. 'Circumcisèd dog' (V.2.351) is as much a gratuitous racial insult as 'thick-lips' (I.1.67). Othello's suicide is a gesture of propitiation to the state whose standards fed his insecurity.

Othello is particularly bleak. No male character begins to examine what lies behind Othello's values. They do not question the rules in the way Hamlet or, more devastatingly, the mad Lear does. Emilia's remarks to Desdemona about wives' behaviour (IV.3.57–102) do open up the possibility of examining the contingent and therefore changeable nature of society, but the most poignant awareness of these shaping forces comes when Bianca acknowledges the limits of her ability to conduct her relationship with Cassio as she would like to. 'I must be circumstanced' (III.4.197), she says. The circumstances are the social and economic forces which give Cassio the power to instruct her to leave him when she is inconvenient, and for him to dictate the times when they can meet. Bianca's awareness of this may be a resigned awareness but at least she does not see it as 'destiny unshunnable'.

There will be nothing in the Lodovico Report to disturb Venice. There will be no examination of what lies behind the way characters are seen and see themselves. The episode was a wicked trick. We shall not have to consider whether Othello would have been justified in killing Desdemona had Cassio really been her lover. We need not wonder if Brabantio would have succeeded in divorcing Desdemona from Othello had it not been for the threatened invasion of Cyprus. And we can certainly drive from our minds the notion that Iago, though unique in his wickedness, was very much a product and reflection of Venetian society. It would take an unconventional production to suggest that the final speech is not leading to a successful political whitewash, an inadequate gloss on what we have seen but a gloss which is necessary for the future stability of the state. Such a production would place Lodovico in a tradition which embraces Fortinbras, Malcolm and Caesar in their suppression of how a thinking audience really responds.

AFTERTHOUGHTS

1

What reasons does Spencer Ellis suggest for Lodovico's 'official whitewash' (page 10) at the end of the play?

2

What disturbs Spencer Ellis about the handling of the Senate scene (Act 1 scene 2) in the two productions he describes?

3

Do you agree with the comment (on Iago) that 'there is not really much evidence to suggest that we have been watching evil incarnate' (page 19)?

4

In what ways does Spencer Ellis suggest that Othello's suicide speech 'embraces those values which have destroyed him' (page 19)? Does this cause you to re-evaluate your view of the play in any way?

Graham Holderness

Graham Holderness is Head of the Drama Department at Roehampton Institute, and has published numerous works of criticism.

ESSAY

Tragedy or satire?

It is an old and familiar question about the artistic and ethical balance of this play: does Iago *cause* the tragedy of Othello and Desdemona, or is he merely the catalyst? Is he a mysteriously potent force of demonic temptation, duping the innocent and leading them to undeserved damnation? Or is he rather an external stimulus, instrumentally necessary for creating the appropriate situation, serviceable in manipulating the victims into their calamitous predicament, but serving in the last instance only to provoke from their own natures the tragic destiny which is their doom and their deserving? Is Iago the 'demi-devil', the 'hellish villain' universally condemned as such at the end of the play; or is the root of the tragedy to be traced through the psychological lineaments of the hero and heroine? Is 'the essential enemy', as F R Leavis put it, 'within the gates'?

In this essay I will concentrate not on Iago but on the characters and relationship of Othello and Desdemona. Let us begin with Othello. We hear much about him from others before he presents himself to the audience, before his peculiar accent of charmed romantic eloquence begins to exert its influence over the reader. In the first scene, both Roderigo and Iago speak of Othello in terms of hatred and insult, in an abusive vocabulary of racist rhetoric: Othello is a 'thick-lips', an 'old black ram', a 'Barbary horse'. The opening dialogue between the two men constructs Othello as something monstrous, bestial, alien, inhuman, detestable.

When Othello appears in person, the contrast between his language and demeanour, and Iago's dehumanising and destructive vituperation, could not be more marked:

> 'Tis yet to know —
> Which, when I know that boasting is an honour,
> I shall provulgate — I fetch my life and being
> From men of royal siege, and my demerits
> May speak unbonneted to as proud a fortune
> As this that I have reached. For know, Iago,
> But that I love the gentle Desdemona,
> I would not my unhousèd free condition
> Put into circumscription and confine
> For the sea's worth . . .
> My parts, my title, and my perfect soul
> Shall manifest me rightly.
>
> (I.2.19–28, 31–32)

Othello's nobility speaks clearly through his magniloquence. But beyond that, it is actually quite difficult to know how to read this language. We could for example read it 'theatrically', assimilating its rhetorical conventions to a certain dramatic style of self-presentation, with our attention focused on what the character is telling us about himself, and not on the fact that it is he himself doing the telling. But if we read it 'psychologically', on the assumption that the style of Othello's utterance is at least as important as its content in revealing the nature of the person, we are bound to be struck by the apparent egotism, pride, even arrogance that distinguish the speech of one who speaks so well, and so beautifully, of his own status and achievements.

On the first type of reading we could note the oddity of Othello's claiming that he won't 'provulgate' his qualities — since that would be boastful — and then proceeding to a full description of his virtues; and we could identify this paradox as a rhetorical convention. On the second type of reading, we would be more likely to identify and judge that trait of 'false modesty' as a fault of character. We might well respond with instinctive dislike to someone who talks with such conceit about his 'perfect soul'. And we are certainly likely to be curious as to how this sublime egotist, who sets himself so clearly apart from the humanity around him, is likely to negotiate the complex relationships with society entailed by his secret marriage to Desdemona.

Is there a hint of regret in Othello's reluctance to compromise his singleness, his distinctive individuality, by linking himself to 'the gentle Desdemona'? We have already observed, in the racialist rhetoric of Iago and Brabantio, what kind of world Othello has to deal with; but we might wonder whether his highminded dignity is a good basis for entering upon such social transactions. That naïve assumption that authority rests in manifest virtue seems oddly askew with the vicious and mercenary plotting that goes on in the dark streets of Venice.

The nature of this initial dramatic contrast between the competitive resentment and malicious plotting of Iago, and the self-absorbed idealising nobility of Othello, creates something of a problem for an audience: for neither of the two perspectives on life, the cynical nor the romantic, seems satisfactory, though each may contain an important degree of truth. Having listened only to Othello's first speeches, we might find ourselves reluctantly forced back to the element of truth in Iago's language. Describing how Othello responded to Iago's application for promotion, the latter comes uncomfortably close to the type of critical response elicited by Othello's own speech and behaviour:

> But he, as loving his own pride and purposes,
> Evades them with a bombast circumstance,
> Horribly stuffed with epithets of war

(I.1.12–14)

It is a harsh and maliciously biased view; but as we have seen, a possible inferential definition of Othello's character. He does appear to love his own pride and purposes; he does speak in an elevated public rhetoric that could be heard as 'bombast'; and he does ground his identity and his judgement in his reputation as a soldier, his experience in war.

When Othello appears before the Venetian council, which is sitting at night discussing the Turkish threat to Cyprus, Brabantio accuses him of stealing his daughter by 'black' magic. It is utterly inconceivable to Brabantio that Desdemona could have entertained a natural passion for a black man. In the certainty of white supremacy, the father has to appeal to notions of witchcraft and enchantment to explain an affection which, in its transgression of paternal authority and racial difference, baffles his imagination: 'For nature so preposterously to err/ ... Sans witchcraft could not' (I.3.62, 64). Othello defends himself and his actions in these terms:

> Rude am I in my speech
> And little blessed with the soft phrase of peace;
> For since these arms of mine had seven years' pith
> Till now some nine moons wasted, they have used
> Their dearest action in the tented field;
> And little of this great world can I speak
> More than pertains to feats of broil and battle;
> And therefore little shall I grace my cause
> In speaking for myself.
>
> (I.3.81–89)

Again we encounter the problem of how to read an accomplished rhetoric of self-presentation. For Othello to claim he is 'rude in his speech' is palpably untrue. The very words in which he protests inarticulacy are beautifully measured and balanced in an eloquent formal verse: the line 'And little blessed with the soft phrase of peace' displays the very elegance of civilised communication it so dishonestly disclaims. If Othello were given a language more appropriate to the soldierly bluntness he is claiming, we would simply accept his utterance as naturalistic self-portraiture: a plain soldier who has no use for courtly eloquence. But since that context of military adventure is described in such elegant verse, using all the skills of a refined poetic idiom, we recognise that something more complex is going on. Othello is not simply explaining to the Venetian government, and incidentally to us, that he is a soldier lacking in communication skills. He seems rather to be constructing his character as an idealised hero of romance, a chivalric adventurer in the mould of Roland or Lancelot, rather than as a professional sixteenth-century man of war.

Brabantio then describes Desdemona, as she appears from his paternalistic point of view:

> A maiden never bold;

Of spirit so still and quiet that her motion
Blushed at herself . . .

(I.3.94–96)

Desdemona's subsequent appearance in person, where she shows
herself to be courageous, independent, strong-willed, outspoken
and unashamed of her potent sexuality, seems to declare
Brabantio's perspective a profound misreading of his daughter's
nature. Surely that image of timid, repressed female subjection
is a patriarchal fantasy, a wish-fulfilment dream of the daughter
Brabantio would wish to have? It certainly bears no resemblance
to the Desdemona we encounter later in the scene:

> My noble father,
> I do perceive here a divided duty:
> To you I am bound for life and education;
> My life and education both do learn me
> How to respect you. You are lord of all my duty,
> I am hitherto your daughter. But here's my husband;
> And so much duty as my mother showed
> To you, preferring you before her father,
> So much I challenge, that I may profess
> Due to the Moor, my lord.

(I.3.178–187)

Yet again, there is a certain oddity in the way this disclosure is
placed within the drama. As so often in *Othello*, where we expect
to find a clear-cut binary opposition, we find something more
complex and elusive. The split between Brabantio's image of
Desdemona as the shy and silent daughter, and our perception of
her as the brave and passionate wife, is clear enough. Now we
might expect to find, corresponding to this opposition, an equally
contradictory antagonism between the father and the lover.
Desdemona's resistance to patriarchal control is articulated by
her as the autonomy of her own preference: she chooses for
herself, and on the basis of that free choice commits herself to
Othello. Is Othello, then, contradistinguished from the father as
an equally unconventional, liberated lover? Not, certainly, in
terms of his own self-image. Explaining Desdemona's passion for
him, Othello recalls the stories of epic adventure, heroic exploit,
manly achievement with which he regaled her:

My story being done,
She gave me for my pains a world of sighs:
She swore, in faith 'twas strange, 'twas passing strange,
'Twas pitiful, 'twas wondrous pitiful;
She wished she had not heard it, yet she wished
That heaven had made her such a man.

(I.3.157–162)

The power Othello exercised over Desdemona is then identical to the power he exercises over the audience: it is rooted in an appeal to the romantic fascination of his military reputation, coded in that characteristically hypnotic eloquence. Desdemona's response to the persuasively recounted tale of Othello's life is one of pity and fear: she feels compassion for his sufferings, and an awe-struck terror of the perils he describes. She almost envies him the freedom of that characteristically masculine, romance world of battles and sieges, accidents and escapes, marvels and terrors; yet an appropriately feminine fear inflects her response towards a decorously female 'pity'. These are of course the tragic emotions, as defined by Aristotle. It is as if Othello is performing to Desdemona, as audience, the tragedy of his own life's adventures, and eliciting from her a cathartic reaction of submissive acceptance. Certainly that almost perverse exchange of fear for love, erotic terror for pitying subjection, is (according to Othello) the basis of their relationship:

She loved me for the dangers I had passed,
And I loved her, that she did pity them.

(I.3.166–167)

Othello's image of the emotionally subjected woman, collapsing into a 'world of sighs' at these tales of the extremity of masculine courage and endurance is not so very far away from Brabantio's vision of his daughter as so submissive that the motion of her own body could make her blush with embarrassment. Although we could hardly be persuaded to accept Brabantio's racist view of the relationship between Othello and Desdemona, we are forced by Othello's own language to concede the element of truth in the father's bewildered interrogation: how could Desdemona 'fall in love with what she feared to look on' (I.3.98)? It is not, as Brabantio blindly imagines, Othello's blackness that incites fear in Desdemona — she seems to attach no significance to his colour. It is rather his masculinity, idealised in the romantic spell of his poetry, that fascinates Desdemona with a fear that entails profound erotic attraction. 'My heart's subdued', she says, begging the Duke to allow her to accompany Othello, 'Even to the utmost pleasure of my lord' (the First Quarto version of this line is surely appropriate in its directness and heavily erotic suggestion; the Folio text, which prints 'very quality' in place of 'utmost pleasure' seems a distinct exercise in toning down). What if the 'utmost pleasure' of her lord were to kill her?

Once Iago's temptation is under way, Othello makes it clear that if he were to be assured of cause for jealousy, he would deal with the matter like the man of action he is:

> I'll see before I doubt; when I doubt, prove;
> And on the proof, there is no more but this:
> Away at once with love or jealousy!
>
> (III.3.188–190)

Faced with her husband's inexplicable rage of jealousy and suspicion, Desdemona also exhibits an attitude of high-minded idealism hopelessly ill-adapted to deal with the complexities of the world she inhabits:

> . . . my love doth so approve him
> That even his stubbornness, his checks, his frowns —
> Prithee, unpin me — have grace and favour in them.
>
> (IV.3.18–20)

Still 'in love with what she feared to look upon', Desdemona displays a romantic purity of emotion verging on the perverse. If the aggressive aspects of Othello's masculinity begin to supersede his chivalric courtliness and to turn on her, that seems to her only an appropriate development of their gender relationship; her duty is to submit in a passive erotic surrender to the hardness of masculine potency.

Othello and Desdemona in Venice are like two aliens ship-wrecked in a strange country, ignorant of the codes and customs, unable to speak or understand the language. Rapt in the oblivion of their romantic idealism, neither is capable of understanding the world of petty jealousy and recrimination, resentment and competition, mean hatred and malicious envy, which surrounds them in the mercenary, utilitarian context of Venetian society.

There is, from one point of view, an enchanting beauty about this idealism, as there is in all romance; and part of the power of the play is to exhibit that beauty in language and action. To see Othello and Desdemona as merely ludicrous, and to turn the play into a kind of dramatic satire (as F R Leavis did in his famous essay 'Diabolic Intellect', in *The Common Pursuit*) is to remain blind to the huge emotional potency of romance. To argue that the beauty of an impassioned idealism is an absurdity is to accept the nature of the world of Venice as it is, and to acknowledge that the only means of survival is the kind of rugged, defensive and vigilant puritanism espoused by Leavis himself.

On the other hand, the play clearly demonstrates not only the perilous ignorance of 'reality' suffered by such idealism, but the internal contradictions which can make romance in itself a dangerous, even death-dealing perversity. When Othello offers his great speech of tribute to Desdemona's fatal beauty ('It is the cause') before he kills her, his poetry comes close to an erotic worship of the dead, the pure and passive female body a perfect emblem of romantic subjection. When Desdemona, dying, tries to exculpate her murderer with her extraordinary line 'Nobody — I myself' (i.e. either she strangled herself, or she invited this tragic destiny by her own acceptance of Othello as her husband) we see her also collaborating in Othello's attempt to hold the purity of their relationship up above the sordid complexities of the world they have struggled to transcend. The same juxtaposition appears in Othello's phrase of self-exculpation, 'an honourable murderer'; and in his last words he still strives to keep his nobility unsoiled by the sordid domestic tragedy of misunderstanding which threatens to engulf it:

> ... in Aleppo once
> Where a malignant and a turbaned Turk
> Beat a Venetian and traduced the state,
> I took by th'throat the circumcisèd dog
> And smote him thus.
> *He stabs himself*

(V.2.348–352)

Othello is simultaneously the malignant foreigner, the hostile alien who has dishonoured the dignity of Venice, and the public-spirited citizen who exacts the state's legitimate penalty. This contradiction between sordid aggression and honourable violence is contained, however, within Venice (the Turks proved, after all, not to be the real enemy), as it is contained within Othello himself. If we continue to the very end to respond to both extremities of that contradiction, we will appreciate *Othello* not as a domestic satire, but as a tragedy of unfulfilled romance.

AFTERTHOUGHTS

Discuss the implications of the title of this essay.

What is *your* reaction to Othello's presentation of himself in the lines quoted by Holderness on pages 24 and 26?

Do you agree with Holderness's interpretation of the basis of Othello's and Desdemona's relationship?

Compare Holderness's view of Othello's and Desdemona's love with that of Cairns (pages 84–94).

Cedric Watts

Cedric Watts is Professor of English at Sussex University, and the author of many scholarly publications.

ESSAY

The semiotics of *Othello*

This essay has three parts. In part 1, I discuss the term 'semiotics'; part 2, I turn to *Othello* the play and Othello the man; and in part 3, I discuss Iago and two critics.

1

'Semiotics' means 'the study of signifying systems'. There are many kinds of signifying systems: language is one great collection of them. Clothes, jewellery, furniture, cars, architecture, paintings: these too can be appraised for what they signify. In *A Theory of Semiotics*, Umberto Eco says: 'Semiotics is in principle the discipline studying everything which can be used in order to lie.'[1] So it's a very large area; one day students may be taking GCSEs and BA degrees in semiotics. Think of the range. Clothes, for instance. If a man wears policeman's uniform, that signifies that he's a policeman; but he might be a lawyer on his way to a fancy-dress party, so the uniform would be ironic; or he might be a bank-robber in disguise, so the uniform would tell a dangerous

---

[1] Umberto Eco, *A Theory of Semiotics* (London, 1977), p. 7.

lie. Thus signs can tell the truth, be ironic, or tell lies. They may sometimes work in reverse: if I know that a prankster has turned a signpost through 180 degrees so that it points away from London instead of towards it, it can still guide me to London.

Michael Riffaterre's book, *Semiotics of Poetry*, says: 'Poetry expresses concepts and things by indirection. To put it simply, a poem says one thing and means another.'[2] He discusses Théophile Gautier's poem, 'In Deserto'. He says that when we first read it, we read it for the obvious sense. Riffaterre calls this the 'heuristic' reading: it delivers the obvious meaning. The poem seems at first to be a description of a desert landscape. But we also notice various oddities: personal references which do not fit this meaning. So we re-read the poem, seeking a deeper significance which will explain those details. He calls this search for the deeper significance the 'hermeneutic' reading. We then find that the poem is not really about the desert landscape; it is really about the plight of the lonely poet who has difficulty in communicating (so he feels as if he's in a wilderness). As we make that discovery, completing the sense of the poem, we find that we can also complete the poem's title: for 'In Deserto' is the latter half of a famous Latin phrase, 'Vox clamans in deserto': 'the voice crying in the wilderness'. So, thanks to this and other examples, Riffaterre can then claim that the *total* significance of a poem is not just the surface meaning elicited by the heuristic reading, nor just the deeper significance revealed by the hermeneutic reading, nor just the two of them together, but the total of both of them *plus* our very activity of working to comprehend the whole: and Riffaterre calls that activity 'the reader's praxis [i.e. practical activity] of the transformation'.[3] (You'll notice that his theory works quite well for some poems, but certainly not for all of them.)

---

[2] Michael Riffaterre, *Semiotics of Poetry* (Bloomington, Ind. and London, 1978), p. 1.
[3] Riffaterre, p. 12.

2

Now what does all that theoretical stuff have to do with
Shakespeare's play *Othello*? Any play uses deceptive and ironic
signs; but *Othello* is more conspicuously sign-conscious than any
other tragedy by Shakespeare. It's full of ironic or reversed
signs.

Consider the storm. There's a tremendous storm at sea
when Othello and the others are voyaging from Venice to Cyprus.
In other Shakespearian tragedies, notably in *Julius Caesar*,
Macbeth and *King Lear*, storms are associated with the disruption
of order among men: moral disorder is accompanied by turmoil
in the heavens. But in *Othello*, the storm is unusual: it's benign
to the protagonists. Though fierce, it scatters the Turkish fleet
which has been threatening Cyprus, and lets the Venetian
voyagers emerge unscathed. This irony is capped near the end of
the play. When Othello kills Desdemona, he says: 'Methinks it
should be now a huge eclipse/ Of sun and moon' (V.2.100–101).
But there's no eclipse; in this very secular tragedy, the skies
remain ironically tranquil.

Here's another instance of reversed signs. The play's chronology is peculiar. The clock moves forwards and backwards. Days
turn into weeks and back again into days; clock-time is reversible
by dialogue. Iago alleges that Desdemona has repeatedly com-
mitted adultery. If his allegation and Othello's consequent
jealousy are to have any credibility, there must be time for
repeated adultery to take place; so it seems that weeks must
have elapsed between Desdemona's arrival on Cyprus and
Othello's jealous conviction that she is guilty. But if you look at
the play's main sequence of days and nights, you find that about
thirty-six hours elapse on Cyprus between her arrival and her
death; she spends with her husband the one full night in that
period. A student once told me that Othello must be incredibly
gullible to believe that the virtuous Desdemona could be
unfaithful. But it's difficult to blame Othello for gullibility when
the audience in the theatre is repeatedly fooled into believing
that her life on Cyprus lasted simultaneously a mere thirty-six
hours *and* several weeks. The so-called 'double time scheme' of

Othello (derided by Thomas Rymer in 1693)[4] proves that the audience can readily be fooled by reversible chronological signs.

Third instance. It's the obvious one. Iago, though utterly dishonest and wicked, is repeatedly called 'honest' and 'good'. Othello, Roderigo, Desdemona, Cassio: they all trust him, even though from the start of the play we know how Machiavellian he is. He appears to bear a deceptive sign inscribed: 'The Honest Iago'. If we look at Othello, we see another paradox. Othello is black (not brown but black), and the text reminds us that in Shakespeare's day 'black' could be a synonym for 'ugly, evil, barbarous, hellish' — as in the words 'O, the more angel she,/ And you the blacker devil!' (V.2.131–132). In Shakespeare's first tragedy, *Titus Andronicus*, the villain is a wicked Moor, Aaron; and he justifies his wickedness by saying that he'll be true to his colour: 'Aaron will have his soul black like his face' (III.1.206). The King in *Love's Labour's Lost* declares: 'Black is the badge of hell' (IV.1.250). The paradox of Othello is that when he first appears in the play he is a living contradiction of all the foul associations of the term. Though he is conspicuously and starkly black amongst all the white people, he immediately proves to be civilised, reasonable, impressively virtuous and responsible; more civilised, indeed, than the Venetian people around him. Instead of joining the brawl in the streets, he contemptuously cries: 'Keep up [i.e. sheathe] your bright swords, for the dew will rust them' (I.2.59). Although assailed by Brabantio's appallingly racist slanders, he remains cool and calm. Accused of winning Desdemona by magic (black magic), he offers a measured and majestic account of his travels and sufferings and of how his life-story had won Desdemona's love; and he calls Desdemona herself to confirm that she chose him freely. Later, he specifically counters the stereotypical association of blackness and lechery ('an old black ram is tupping your white ewe') by saying that if he wishes Desdemona to accompany him to Cyprus, it is:

> not
> To please the palate of my appetite;
> Nor to comply with heat — the young affects

---

[4] Thomas Rymer, *A Short View of Tragedy* (London and Baldwin, 1693), pp. 120–123.

In me defunct — and proper satisfaction;
But to be free and bounteous to her mind.

(I.3.258–262)

Next, he seems to be a living contradiction of the association of blackness with hell and devilry. He's a Christian convert; a valued servant of the Venetian state — a Christian state. On Cyprus, when a brawl instigated by Iago occurs, Othello says:

Are we turned Turks and to ourselves do that
Which heaven hath forbid the Ottomites?
For Christian shame, put by this barbarous brawl.

(II.3.164–166)

The Europeans are behaving like barbarians, and the black Othello has to remind them to behave like Christians and not like the Turkish enemy, the infidels.

The more attentive we are to the ironic and reversed signs of the play, the more significant will be the manner of Othello's eventual suicide. Here are his words:

When you shall these unlucky deeds relate
Speak of me as I am: nothing extenuate,
Nor set down aught in malice. Then must you speak
Of one that loved not wisely, but too well;
Of one, not easily jealous but, being wrought,
Perplexed in the extreme; of one whose hand
Like the base Indian threw a pearl away
Richer than all his tribe; of one whose subdued eyes,
Albeit unusèd to the melting mood,
Drop tears as fast as the Arabian trees
Their med'cinable gum. Set you down this:
And say, besides, that in Aleppo once
Where a malignant and a turbaned Turk
Beat a Venetian and traduced the state,
I took by th'throat the circumcisèd dog
And smote him thus.
    He stabs himself

(V.2.337–352)

That speech, by the broken Othello, should remind us of his first great speech of self-justification before the Senators of Venice.

There's the same elaborate determination to set the record straight: to specify the reading of Othello's character that Othello wants others to adopt. Then there's the so-called 'Othello music':[5] sonorous, majestic, tinged with the exotic. The General who once talked of the Anthropophagi, the Propontic, the Hellespont, here talks of the Arabian trees that shed medicinal gum. This 'Othello music' resembles in quality Christopher Marlowe's powerful lines (like 'And ride in triumph through Persepolis'):[6] exotic place-names and polysyllables add to the weighty rhythmic surge; and, in Othello's case, those place-references invoke regions where the map of the real world blends into a map of a legendary world of myth and magic. For semioticians there is special richness in the last few lines of Othello's speech. Consider the kind of stabbing gesture that the actor eventually has to make. To fit the sense of the lines, the gesture would have to be a large zigzag, going away from Othello towards the imagined Turk and then back again and into Othello: a most conspicuous reversed sign. The stabbing of the imagined enemy of the Venetian state becomes the stabbing of the defender of the state. The image of the exotic foe, and the contrasting image of the defender of European civilisation, suddenly merge. Aggressor and defender, infidel and Christian, barbarian and Venetian, fuse in death, impaled on one blade. Othello has revealed for sign-readers the main cause of his downfall: the cultural and psychological insecurity of a man caught between two worlds and belonging fully to neither; a self crushed between conflicting stereotypes; a man whose insecurity had been goaded into violence by racial prejudice. After his death, we see the ultimate reversed sign of the play: a double bed which has become a bier: a bed for newly-weds which has become the resting-place of two corpses, one black, one white, united in death.

---

[5] See G Wilson Knight, *The Wheel of Fire* (London, 1960), chap. 5.
[6] Christopher Marlowe, *The Complete Plays*, edited by J B Steane (Harmondsworth, 1969), p. 129.

3

'I am not what I am,' says Iago. Since his avowed motives are numerous and not fully consistent, any reading of his character has to move (in Riffaterre's terms) from the heuristic to the hermeneutic. Consciously or not, we are semioticians when we analyse him. What we then find, rather alarmingly, is that Iago is himself a semiotician — of a very cynical kind. Iago has a radically cynical outlook, but enough intelligence to see that the world offers evidence to refute a cynic. Evidence, for example, that love can triumph over prejudice: Desdemona's love for Othello is the radiant example. So what Iago repeatedly does is this: he seeks to transform the world so that it vindicates cynicism. He is an expert in 'the praxis of the transformation': paradoxical transformation. Roderigo is a spineless wooer; Iago will manipulate and goad him to the point where the spineless Roderigo finds himself attacking Cassio. Cassio is an 'arithmetician' and a courtly gentleman skilled in social graces; so Iago converts him, for a while, into a drunken sot. Desdemona is conspicuously loving and chaste; so Iago will 'turn her virtue into pitch', converting her, in her husband's imagination, into a lecherous whore. Othello initially is a living refutation of the notion that blacks are barbarians; but Iago's scheme reduces Othello to the point at which, barbarically, he cries, 'I'll chop her into messes!' What gives much of the power to Iago's plot is racial prejudice: his own, and that of others.

One of the cruellest ironies in the whole play is that Desdemona's transcendence of racial prejudice is used by Iago, crucially, as evidence that she is likely to betray Othello. In Act III scene 3, to tempt Othello into suspicion of Desdemona, Iago's method is to argue on these lines: 'Your reading of Desdemona as virtuous and faithful is superficial; it's merely heuristic. You should note this oddity, the tell-tale anomaly; in marrying you she betrayed her father and her white race. Then, you should be led to the hermeneutic significance, which is that she is radically treacherous; so she is capable of betraying her husband (particularly as it's unnatural for white to marry black).' Shakespeare thus criticises Riffaterre's *Semiotics of Poetry* 370 years before that book appeared, by suggesting that sometimes the heuristic reading may be the true reading, while the hermeneutic reading may offer only an illusory significance. Alas, Othello proves too receptive a pupil of Iago, and soon believes a fatally hermeneutic interpretation of a lost handkerchief. As Rymer drily commented, 'Had it been Desdemona's Garter, the Sagacious Moor might have smelt a Rat.'[7]

In 1904, A C Bradley, in *Shakespearean Tragedy*, gave a warmly sympathetic account of Othello's character; and, to support that account, he naturally put much of the blame for the tragic outcome upon Iago, by emphasising Iago's cunning.[8] In 1952, F R Leavis, in *The Common Pursuit*, attacked Bradley by claiming that 'Bradley's Othello is, rather, Othello's';[9] in other words, Bradley's account of Othello endorses Othello's view of himself. For Leavis, the source of the tragedy lay in Othello's egotism, evident in his habit of 'self-approving self-dramatisation'. To support his unsympathetic appraisal of Othello, Leavis naturally discounted the skill of Iago, asserting that Iago was 'merely ancillary' to the plot-mechanism. Feminist students today tend to be readily receptive to Leavis's view, since Othello not only trusts Iago rather than his own wife but also, after her death, seems more concerned to assert the merits of Othello than to mourn his murder of an innocent woman. Certainly Bradley's reading of Othello now seems rather sentimental. Perhaps, however, Leavis's Othello is, rather, Iago's; particularly when Leavis remarks that the Moor's colour 'emphasiz[es] the disparity of the match'. Step back from Leavis's interpretation, think of the visual force of the stage-play, and you may form a more accurate interpretation of the central sign: a black man among whites. Othello, as his blackness reminds us, has good reason for feeling culturally insecure; good reason for some compensatory self-dramatisation. Paul Robeson, the black singer who acted well the role of Othello, once said: 'But the colour is essentially secondary — except as it emphasises the difference in *culture*. This is the important thing.'[10] The point is *not* that one should 'make allowances' for a black man: to do so would be racially

---

[7] Rymer, p. 140.

[8] A C Bradley: *Shakespearean Tragedy* [1904] (London, 1957), esp. pp. 190–194.

[9] F R Leavis, *The Common Pursuit* [1952] (Harmondsworth, 1962), p. 141.

[10] Quoted in *Marxists on Literature*, edited by David Craig (Harmondsworth, 1975), p. 113.

condescending. The point is that Othello's colour reminds us that his homeland is neither Morocco, which he left so long ago, nor Europe, where racial prejudice can be openly voiced against him; he is culturally divided and insecure, and is therefore vulnerable to Iago's semiotic manipulation. Accordingly, one semiotic interpretation of Desdemona's death is that it results from the racism which Othello has experienced and which Iago deftly exploits. Another interpretation, however, is that (as Emilia indicates at IV.2.85–102) Desdemona is ultimately a victim of the stereotyping of women by men, a stereotyping in which numerous men, whether black or white, connive. Either way, the play proves remarkably up to date in inviting us to make a critically hermeneutic reading of the stereotypes of race and gender. *Othello* teaches semiotics while offering warnings against the seductions of semiotics. Iago, a seductively corrupt teacher, finally attempts to defeat any semiotician by remaining obdurately silent about his ultimate motive. And Othello's poetry, at its most lucidly majestic, implicitly mocks the jargon ('heuristic', 'hermeneutic', 'praxis of the transformation') of modern literary theories.

AFTERTHOUGHTS

1

Trace the importance to the argument of this essay of the ideas presented in Riffaterre's *Semiotics of Poetry*. What poems would *not* respond to analysis along the lines described by Riffaterre (page 34)?

2

What significance does Watts attach to the systems of 'reversed signs' examined on pages 35–38?

3

Do you agree with Watts's argument that Iago 'is himself a semiotician' (page 39)?

4

What has learning about semiotics taught you about *Othello*?

Brean Hammond

Brean Hammond is Professor of English at Aberystwyth University, and is the author of numerous scholarly publications.

ESSAY

'Silence that dreadful bell': *Othello* and critical neurosis

What you are about to read is more a *confession* than a critical essay. All teachers who write or lecture resemble patients on a psychoanalyst's couch, a point made by the French writer Roland Barthes with customary wit and vigour in his essay 'Writers, Intellectuals, Teachers':

> Imagine that I am a teacher: I speak, endlessly, in front of and for someone who remains silent. I am the person who says I . . . I am the person who, under cover of *setting out* a body of knowledge, *puts out* a discourse, *never knowing how that discourse is being received* and thus forever forbidden the reassurance of a definitive image — even if offensive — which would *constitute* me. In the *exposé*, more aptly named than we tend to think, it is not knowledge which is exposed, it is the subject (who exposes himself to all sorts of painful adventures). The mirror is empty, reflecting back to me no more than the falling away of my language as it gradually unrolls. Like the Marx Brothers disguised as Russian airmen (in *A Night at the Opera* . . .) I am, at the beginning of my exposé, rigged out with a large false beard which, drenched little by little with the flood

of my own words . . . I then feel coming unstuck piecemeal in front of everybody.[1]

What I want to confess is that I have never *liked* Shakespeare's *Othello*. For a Professor of English Literature, not liking anything Shakespeare wrote virtually constitutes gross moral turpitude, grounds for instant dismissal from my post — so ingrained in our culture is the love of Shakespeare, so close to idolatry our reverential respect for our great national bard. Shakespeare is such a powerful cultural icon that it is difficult to know whether not liking one of his great tragedies is a personal neurosis, some kind of private dementia, or whether it can be rationalised as an 'objective' critical position for which there are at least some arguments. That is what I want to explore in this essay. Can I liberate myself at last from the guilt caused by repression of my dislike for one of Shakespeare's greatest plays? Can a psychological problem be redefined as a critical one?

Let me regress to the year 1963 when, at the age of twelve, I first heard of *Othello*. I had been chosen to be a producer's assistant at a school production of the play. My main task was to ring the bell that sounds so deafeningly during the riot scene (II.3) when Cassio and Montano are brawling. Othello's line 'Silence that dreadful bell: it frights the isle/ From her propriety' (II.3.169–170) was my cue to stop ringing the bell, but in the fearful clamour, I could never hear the cue and kept on ringing the bell. Every night Othello had to repeat the cue at least twice and every night I was set upon savagely by irate stage-hands intent on suppressing the bell. Ever since then, my relationship to the play has been a complex one.

Even at the tender age of twelve, certain aspects of the play's plot, characterisation and stage-craft failed to add up for me. Why, in the space of some ninety lines from Iago's 'Ha! I like not that (III.3.35), should Othello be giving him (his inferior in social and military rank) *carte blanche* to blacken his new wife's name? 'If thou dost love me,/ Show me thy thought' (III.3.114–115) and: 'Nay, yet there's more in this./ I prithee

---

[1] Roland Barthes, 'Writers, Intellectuals, Teachers' (1971), reprinted in *Image, Music, Text* edited by Stephen Heath (1977, rep. Oxford, 1984), p. 194.

speak to me as to thy thinkings,/ As thou dost ruminate, and give thy worst of thoughts/ The worst of words' (III.3.129–132). If I had been writing this play, I mused, I would have had Othello say, 'Seal up thy lips, thou varlet, if thou think'st,/ Aught unbeseeming to my lovely wife' and would then have had Othello take the matter up in private with Desdemona. Equally puzzling to my youthful brain was the piece of plotting that has Emilia stealing the handkerchief for Iago. Why does this loyal, good-natured and trustworthy servant *do* such a thing? She is herself conscious of the difficulty here:

> My wayward husband hath a hundred times
> Wooed me to steal it; but she so loves the token —
> For he conjured her she should ever keep it —
> That she reserves it evermore about her
> To kiss and talk to. I'll have the work ta'en out,
> And give't Iago.
> What he will do with it, heaven knows, not I.
>
> (III.3.289–295)

There is only one thing an honest man *can* do with a hand-kerchief, my juvenile common sense asserted, and that is to blow his nose on it. In the scene immediately following (III.4), Emilia's action comes under severe strain as Desdemona, intensely anxious about the loss of the handkerchief, asks Emilia where she might have mislaid it. Emilia, fully aware of its importance to her mistress, replies with a direct lie — 'I know not, madam' (line 24). When Othello enters, it becomes clear that the hand-kerchief is for him no trivial item. To say that it has sentimental value, even symbolic significance, is to understate the case. Othello regards it with awe — 'there's magic in the web of it' (line 69) — and his account of how it came into his possession suddenly introduces an entirely new texture into the play. This clear-headed general, master military tactician and forthright fighting man, has a mother who was in touch with Egyptian 'charmers', prophetic 200-year-old sibyls and holy silkworms. And he believes it all.

Watching even our amateurish production of this, I could sense the change in atmosphere, the extraordinary charge produced by the convergence of two different worlds. If ownership of the handkerchief has been transferred from Othello to Iago, as we know it has, he will believe that Iago has found a form of black magic more potent than the tutelary magic protecting him. Yet, party to all this, Emilia says not a word about its whereabouts. She might have said: 'Good sir, be content; use your wife not so./ She dropped the napkin mopping up your brow/ And now it safe within my chamber lies.' I recall that during the rehearsals for our production, the actors did seek direction on this point, and I remember the director making the valid point that there is a *sub-text* underneath this (that is to say, a motivation which is not explicitly announced in the text). Desdemona has claimed in lines 27–28 that Othello is not jealous. Possibly this goads Emilia into keeping silent, since she judges all men by her husband's standards, and wants to prove her idealistic mistress a ninny. Once they have witnessed the intensity of Othello's concern for it, Emilia's inaction may plausibly be explained by fright: how can she admit she has it after a scene like that? Even if we can find some psychologically convincing account of Emilia's deceit here, however, it doesn't quite solve the problem, because it can't be made to square with a *functional* analysis of her role. Having formed certain expectations of Emilia based on her costume, language, stage-behaviour — all the various means by which 'character' is transmitted to an audience — we construe her as a faithful servant and companion to Desdemona, though her view of sexual mores is a good deal more robust, and of the male gender less idealistic than that of her mistress. Thus, it is she who exposes Iago's plot; and her devotion to Desdemona has given her the right to shriek outspoken vituperation of Othello: 'Nay, lay thee down and roar,/ For thou hast killed the sweetest innocent/ That e'er did lift up eye' (V.2.197–199). On the other hand, we have seen that it is her dishonesty more than anything else that furnishes Othello with the 'ocular proof' upon which he condemns Desdemona. She seems to act 'out of character', failing to observe the stage conventions through which we understand her role.

Some years after the school production of *Othello*, in 1970 to be exact, *Othello* was one of the texts I studied at Edinburgh University in the second year of my degree course in English. I discovered that the play was based on the seventh story in the third decade of Giraldi Cinthio's *Hecatommithi*, an Italian romance published in Venice in 1565. This was part of a wider discovery, that one tactic in Shakespeare criticism was to compare Shakespeare's plays with the originals on which they were based, usually with the intention of pointing out how Shakespeare's modifications had enriched the originals. In Cinthio, Emilia does not steal the handkerchief; Iago does. I venture to think that Shakespeare should not have altered this from the source, because in transferring the responsibility to Emilia, he not only forces her to act uncharacteristically but he made *sheer luck* the linchpin of the tragedy. This change is part of a very much more significant alteration in the role of Iago, which deserves comment. In Cinthio, Iago was a relatively straightforward case of unrequited lust. He loved Desdemona and, because she did not return his feelings, he fancied that she must love someone else (namely, Cassio) and turned his attention to revenge. There is, in Cinthio, the reductiveness and direct-ness typical of the romance form, where time is seldom wasted on psychological nicety:

> The wicked ensign, caring nothing for the loyalty due to his wife or the friendship, loyalty, and duty he owed to the Moor, fell passionately in love with Disdemona and turned all his thoughts to seeing whether he might enjoy her. But he was anxious not to reveal himself, fearing that he might meet sudden death if the Moor should find out. He sought by secret devious ways to bring it to the notice of the lady that he loved her; but she had only the Moor in her thoughts, and gave no thought to the ensign or to anyone else. Everything that the ensign did to kindle in her a love for him was useless. So he imagined that the reason was that Disdemona had become enamoured of the captain and so decided to put him out of the way. Furthermore he changed the love that he bore the lady into the bitterest hatred, and pondered how he might arrange that, once the captain was killed, if he could not enjoy Disdemona himself, the Moor might also be prevented from enjoying her either.[2]

In Shakespeare, the essential simplicity of 'he changed the love that he bore the lady into the bitterest hatred' is not

---

[2] Reprinted in the Arden edition of *Othello* edited by M R Ridley (1958, rep. London and New York, 1979), p. 239.

adequate. Very early on Iago is given grounds for hating Othello and Cassio, in that the former has chosen the latter as his Lieutenant. Cassio is, in Iago's opinion, a Sandhurst product who has seen no active service: a gentleman-officer more suited to court flattery than soldiership, whose 'effeminate' manners do not sort with the brittle definition of masculinity that Iago presumably entertains. Like many of Shakespeare's soldiers, Iago perceives soldiery and heterosexual relationships as mutually exclusive realms of human experience. Liking women, courting them, considering them as having something valuable to say, he regards as weakness. (Some critics and directors have speculated that his bluff maleness conceals homosexual urges.) In a later monologue, Iago offers up so many motives for his malicious behaviour that they cease to function as genuine motives and are more adequately construed as symptoms of some kind of psychopathology: in the space of twenty-five lines (II.1.277–303), Iago tells us that he thinks Cassio loves Desdemona and quite possibly she returns it. He himself 'loves' her both out of lust and out of an instinct of vengeance, since he suspects that Othello may have cuckolded him with Emilia: and for good measure, he throws in the suspicion that Cassio may have cuckolded him as well. What are we to make of all of this? How are we to understand the role of Iago? Coleridge's apt comment on this soliloquy (he calls it 'the motive-hunting of motiveless malignity') suggests that it does not offer any *explanation* of Iago's conduct, but rather exemplifies the curious psychological quirk that, no matter how uncontainedly wicked individuals can be, they always need to excuse their conduct or to justify it to themselves. Recently, I have encountered a linguistic/semiotic analysis of this speech, which tries to explain why it has such a slippery effect:

> ... the levels of Iago's utterances shift continuously, even when the referential axis appears to be the same, because he opens onto the real action an imaginary backcloth within the theatre of *his* mind, no less than in the shifts of interpretation into which he forces his interlocutors ... Iago spins his web not through the stability of the subject and the predication of a purpose, but through the very sliding, curiously decentred, of the enunciation, in a tangled syntax in which meaning never

reaches firm ground but is consumed, mixed and overturned, without finding an *enounce* on which to rest.[3]

Though I hadn't the benefit of Serpieri's work as an undergraduate, and hadn't heard of 'semiotics' or 'enounces', my reading around the play for the purposes of essay-writing uncovered the fact that many critics have expressed reservations about Iago's role. Some do not actually regard him as a 'character' in quite the sense that we use the term. Bernard Spivack, for instance, in *Shakespeare and the Allegory of Evil* (1958) suggested that Iago was to be understood as the descendant of the Vice in the medieval Morality play, the intriguer who, though seemingly devoted to the welfare of his friend, is in reality bent on precipitating his ruin. F R Leavis's famous essay 'Diabolic Intellect and the Noble Hero' gave some respectability to my own doubts by arguing that Iago is merely some kind of mental projection of Othello. According to Leavis, previous critics, and in particular A C Bradley, had been naïvely sentimental in their view of *Othello*. Othello is only ostensibly valiant and upright: actually, as his manner of speaking and his posturing behaviour proves, he is overblown, self-serving and odious. The play is actually about Othello, who is not what he appears, and Iago is 'merely a necessary piece of dramatic machinery'.[4] Leavis is now considered a doubtful ally and the young critic on the make is wise not to identify too closely with his opinions. Leavis was not arguing, as I am, that the play has structural faults. He was arguing that the Bard had once again outsmarted all his critics (except Leavis) in camouflaging Othello's true character under what Leavis, following G Wilson Knight, dubbed 'the Othello music'. Christopher Norris has pointed out in a recent article that Leavis's refutation of Bradley here, the cynic confronting the idealist, is actually a replay of the Othello–Iago duel in the play.[5] This argument was important

---

[3] Alessandro Serpieri, 'Reading the Signs: towards a Semiotics of Shakespearan Drama', in *Alternative Shakespeares*, edited by John Drakakis (London and New York, 1985), pp. 138–139. Translated by Keir Elam.

[4] F R Leavis, 'Diabolic Intellect and the Noble Hero', in *The Common Pursuit* (London, 1952), pp. 136–159.

[5] Christopher Norris, 'Post-Structuralist Shakespeare: Text and Ideology', in *Alternative Shakespeares*, pp. 47–66.

to me, as it has been to all those who have read it, but it is not now my opinion. At the same time as discovering Leavis, I discovered Thomas Rymer, who, according to the essay question I had to answer, had called the play 'a Bloody Farce, without salt or savour'. Now *this*, I thought, was promising, so I rushed to the library to find a copy of Rymer's 1692–93 essay *A Short View of Tragedy*.

I found in Rymer an energetic and passionate critic of the play, who has an amusing, if heavy-handed, line in irony. Offering a sceptical plot summary, Rymer comments:

> What ever rubs or difficulty may stick on the Bark, the Moral, sure, of this Fable is very instructive.
>
> 1. First, This may be a caution to all Maidens of Quality how, without their Parents consent, they run away with Blacka-moors . . .
>
> Secondly, This may be a warning to all good Wives, that they look well to their Linnen.
>
> Thirdly, This may be a lesson to Husbands, that before their Jealousie be Tragical, the proofs be Mathematical.[6]

The limitations in Rymer's rigid late-seventeenth-century neo-classicism were not too difficult, even for an undergraduate, to perceive. He was a thoroughgoing Aristotelian, who considered the most important part of the drama to be the 'fable' (what we would call the plot), which he thought should inculcate an obvious morality (he invented the formula 'poetic justice'). 'Decorum', the relationship between social rank and moral conduct, was for him an unbendable principle of dramatic characterisation: in an earlier treatise called *The Tragedies of the Last Age* (1677) he makes a typically limited remark on the dramatic portrayal of kings: 'we are to presume the greatest virtues, where we find the highest of rewards, and though it is not necessary that all *Heroes* should be Kings, yet undoubtedly all crown'd heads by *Poetical right* are *Heroes*'.[7] (Where does this

---

[6] Thomas Rymer, *A Short View of Tragedy* (1693), reprinted in *The Critical Works of Thomas Rymer* edited and introduced by Curt A Zimansky (New Haven, 1956), p. 132.

[7] Rymer, *The Critical Works*, p. 42.

leave Macbeth or Lear?) Running through his commentary on *Othello* is what appears to be racial prejudice, but is perhaps more accurately a rigid sense of decorum, which prevents him from believing that Desdemona, a Senator's Daughter, *could conceivably* love a non-Caucasian. Even more profoundly shocking to modern readers was Rymer's view of Shakespeare's language. Glorious metaphorical richness was treated by Rymer as sheer bombast. (I was to learn that, in this, Rymer was expressing a distrust of metaphorical figuration that had become very general in his time.) When I handed in my essay, my tutor informed me archly that no one was inclined to take Rymer seriously nowadays. Indeed, he offered me J W H Atkins's study of *English Literary Criticism* in the period (an illustrious predecessor to me in my present post!) in which Atkins quotes with approbation Macaulay's description of Rymer as 'the worst critic that ever lived'. My essay didn't get a high mark!

But I thought then, and I think now, that Rymer had some valuable points. Let's return, briefly, to the issue of decorum. Historians of criticism use Rymer, as we have seen, to represent the mechanical, prescriptive following of Aristotelian 'rules' that disfigures neo-classical thinking about literature. This is, however, a caricature of the truth. Take the case of Iago, for instance. For Rymer, the dramatic portrayal of a *soldier* was, and had to be, the portrayal of a character 'open-hearted, frank, plain-dealing . . . a character constantly worn by them for some thousands of years in the World' whereas Iago is a 'close, dissembling, false, insinuating rascal'.[8] A typical response to Rymer here would be that Shakespeare's greatness precisely lies in the extent to which he sees *individuals* rather than types. Without concern for dramatic tradition, Shakespeare has, with superior realism and fidelity to experience, shown us that soldiers like Iago, who bluster, swear, cheat and lie, do exist. And the character is all the more forceful because it works *against* long-established conceptions of the soldier's bearing. Yet we have already had cause to wonder whether Iago is in any sense a 'realistic' character. We talk, in ordinary parlance, of films or television plays being more or less 'realistic', more or

---

[8] Rymer, *The Critical Works*, p. 135.

less 'plausible'. It seems to be an important criterion of the success of some, not of all, artistic events. But it is very difficult to say what is meant by this, and what has been meant by this historically. For Rymer, the characters in *Othello* were not plausible, were not realistic, because he negotiated the plausible and the real by means of certain notions of decorum. We still *do* operate with (doubtless different) conceptions of decorum, and the measuring of artistic representation against 'real life' is still not straightforward. I have heard the soap-opera *Neighbours* being dismissed as 'unrealistic', which turned out to mean that the ratio between screen-time and significant incident was unconvincingly high. 'Real life', the critic felt, is not lived on such a constant level of crisis. What does it mean, then, to say that Iago is 'realistic'? In life, individuals often get disgruntled when their career advancement is blocked and the boss chooses the wrong deputy, but they do not, as a rule, plot to ruin the lives of all those connected with him. To Rymer, Iago's conduct was so extreme that he ceased to carry conviction as a *representative* figure. Desdemona is another case. For Rymer, convinced that it is the duty of 'poetry' to be more 'philosophical' than history (that is to say, for art not to render life faithfully but to *improve* upon it), the poet must represent on stage only modest women, and Desdemona's conduct is not modest. Again, the simple answer is that Desdemona is a *real* woman. Shakespeare disregards decorum in the interests of greater imaginative truth. Yet clearly, there is something unconvincing, improbable, in the knack she has of talking to Othello about Cassio at precisely the wrong moment. Actually she does meddle in affairs that are not strictly speaking her business and her timing is lousy. This is as much a necessity of the plot, of the building of suspense, as it is an expression of character. Questions of convention, dramatic realism and plausibility are not so easy to determine, and it is not self-evident that Rymer has it wrong.

Since the eighteenth century, critics have tended to celebrate Shakespeare for aspects of his writing *other than* his plots, which have come to seem unimportant: mere vehicles for the beauties of the language and the subtleties of characterisation. Rymer directs our attention valuably back to the 'fable', which to him is quite inseparable from characterisation. You can't have convincing characters in a weak plot because plot just *is* character in action. This is not a tenable view of every play, but arguably plot is more important to *Othello* than to Shakespeare's other major tragedies because beside them it is, crudely, a kitchen-sink drama. Rymer frequently bashes contemporary plays over the head with ancient Greek plays because the latter have a metaphysical dimension. Their plots heighten pity because the protagonist is usually an innocent victim of the gods. Clearly, there are Shakespearean tragedies in which this classical possibility is canvassed, though never with unequivocal endorsement — but *Othello* is not one of them. The plot is what Seymour Chatman would classify as a 'plot of character', depicting a process of deteriorating change in the moral character of the protagonist as revealed in his actions and feelings, the change precipitated by a scheming antagonist.[9] Elements of *suspense* loom large: since we know what Iago is about, the whole play is built on dramatic irony. The audience's superior knowledge produces deep anxiety about the outcome for those characters with whom we sympathise. The play does not concern itself very significantly with fate or destiny (though some critical accounts try to introduce such a dimension through Othello's preoccupation with magic and sorcery); and Rymer's point that the play has no convincing moral has been re-cast by more recent critics who have not found in it any profitable doctrine. One clear line in twentieth-century criticism of *Othello*, leading from A C Bradley to Harley Granville-Barker to Wilson Knight to F R Leavis, is that the play is a meaningless tragedy in which the protagonist's dire destiny is fulfilled without any appreciable gain in self-knowledge. Othello's final soliloquy:

> Whip me, ye devils,
> From the possession of this heavenly sight!
> Blow me about in winds! Roast me in sulphur!
> Wash me in steep-down gulfs of liquid fire!
>
> (V.2.275–278)

has been described acidly by F R Leavis as 'an intolerably intensified form of the common "I could kick myself"'.[10]

---

[9] Seymour Chatman, *Story and Discourse: Narrative Structure in Fiction and Film* (Ithaca and London, 1978, rep. 1983), p. 48.
[10] In 'Diabolic Intellect and the Noble Hero', *The Common Pursuit*, p. 150.

Even for those who do not require of tragedy that the protagonist should experience any gain in self-knowledge or that it should promote any doctrine at all, the play's plot, on which as I have argued, it is more than usually dependent, must be something of an embarrassment. As Rymer was the first to point out, time in *Othello* is measured by two different and incompatible clocks. If we take the play's chronology literally, then it follows, as Rymer points out, that there has scarcely been any time for Desdemona to get involved with Cassio:

> *Michael Cassio* came not from *Venice* in the Ship with *Desdemona*, nor till this Morning could be suspected of an opportunity with her. And 'tis now but Dinner time; yet the *Moor* complains of his Fore-head. He might have set a Guard on *Cassio*, or have lockt up *Desdemona*, or have observ'd their carriage a day or two longer. He is on other occasions phlegmatick enough: this is very hasty.[11]

But if one series of time-references establishes the action as continous from the arrival in Cyprus to the murder of Desdemona, another set of references studded through Act III and continuing into IV and V suggest that considerable time must have elapsed between the arrival in Cyprus and the events that precipitate the tragedy commencing in Act III. One example of the longer time-scale is Othello's exchange with Iago in III.3:

> What sense had I of her stolen hours of lust?
> I saw't not, thought it not, it harmed not me.
> I slept the next night well, was free and merry.
> I found not Cassio's kisses on her lips.

> (III.3.335–338)

The double-time scale, and the speeding up of the action from Act III onwards, which results in Othello's jealousy being very rapidly aroused, may not seem a very significant problem. After all, most decent plays set up some fairly complicated interaction between performance time (the time it takes for the play to be acted in the theatre), plot time (the temporal sequence in the

---

[11] Rymer, *The Critical Works*, p. 150.

way events are revealed to the audience) and chronological time (the 'real' historical period covered by a slice of dramatic action). As long ago as 1849–50, 'Christopher North' argued in *Blackwood's Magazine* that Shakespeare deliberately employed the double calendar as part of his conscious artistry, a view taken by M R Ridley, editor of the Arden edition:

> [Shakespeare] knew to a fraction of an inch how far he could go in playing a trick on his audience, and the measure of his success is precisely the unawareness of the audience in the theatre that any trick is being played. What Shakespeare is doing is to present, before our eyes, an unbroken series of events happening in 'short time', but to present them against a background of events not presented but implied, which gives the needed impression of 'long time'.[12]

I find myself unconvinced by an explanation which smacks somewhat of bardolatry. Rather, I suspect that the double calendar exposes an insecurity in characterisation, a measure of doubt about the nature of Othello's passion. Can a passion of such intensity be supposed to develop within the telescoped time necessary to a convincing portrayal of it, or do we need to presume that it has matured gradually? Is this jealousy of Othello's a function of the immaturity of his relationship with Desdemona, or of its complacency? Shakespeare gives the whole process of Othello's jealousy from conception to execution in a single scene, yet seems uncertain about the plausibility of this. Othello the noble, upright, self-possessed military leader, the loving husband of a virtuous wife, is persuaded to murder by a transparent hypocrite whose claim to 'honesty' must surely be seen through in the very activities he undertakes to prove it. There is, in short, a problem of belief in the play. Sir Michael Redgrave once refused to play the part of Othello because, he said, he was 'too rational to understand all that jealousy'. Perhaps that is my problem too.

From the vantage-point of the present. I will conclude with a few further words of self-reflection. Currently, progressive interest in Shakespeare is less in re-reading Shakespeare's

---

[12] M R Ridley, in the Arden *Othello*, p. ixx.

meaning than in re-reading the meaning of 'Shakespeare'. Two volumes of essays published in 1985, *Political Shakespeare* and *Alternative Shakespeares*, made a considerable impact by canvassing the view that Shakespeare's prime position in the literary league is not, or not simply, a function of his inherent genius. Alan Sinfield, in *Political Shakespeare*:

> Shakespeare's construction in English culture generally as the great National Poet whose plays embody universal truths has led to his being used to underwrite established practices in literary criticism and, consequently, in examinations ... For literary criticism, Shakespeare is the keystone which guarantees the ultimate stability and rightness of the category 'Literature'.[13]

James Kavanagh, in *Alternative Shakespeares*, puts the point in another way:

> The word 'Shakespeare' is less the name of a specific historical figure, than a sign that has come to designate a vaguely defined, but fiercely defended, set of characteristics that function as the touchstone of value for what we commonly call the 'English literary tradition'.[14]

I have written this piece because I think it may be valuable to provide an example of *negative* criticism for readers who are all too often given the impression that it is unacceptable to express reservations about great literary masterpieces. Though this piece is conventional in its technique — perhaps very conventional, given that it is an exercise in evaluation — there is a radical political valency in what it attempts to do. My essay questions some of the 'universal truths' that *Othello* is said to communicate, and it does so by using what I recognise to be a partly reductive, infuriatingly common-sensical approach that is thought to be the outmoded property of the seventeenth century. Sometimes, however, it is more radical to return to neglected

---

[13] Alan Sinfield, 'Give an Account of Shakespeare and Education etc.', in *Political Shakespeare: New Essays in Cultural Materialism* edited by Jonathan Dollimore and Alan Sinfield (Manchester, 1985), p. 135.
[14] James H Kavanagh, 'Shakespeare in Ideology', in *Alternative Shakespeares*, p. 144.

critical approaches than to invent new ones. Shakespeare was a writer for the stage who would not have recognised himself in the designation 'man of letters'. Yet by the later eighteenth century, and very obviously in the nineteenth, criticism was biased against stage representation of Shakespeare. Only reading, it was thought, could do justice to the inexhaustible complexity of his plays; the reader's imagination was the only theatre comprehensive enough to stage his work. Tawdry theatrical trappings, the necessity to make reductive directorial decisions, could only impoverish him. Within such an aesthetic, Shakespeare's plots came to seem unimportant, part of the melodramatic mechanics, the body that imprisons the spiritual soul of poetic language. *Othello* in the study, where language can be abstracted from the flux of performance, is a very different kind of animal from the play as experienced by an audience demanding to be convinced of its emotional logic. My essay attempts to re-think the purely theatrical aspects of *Othello*'s plot and to exhume Rymer's point about the interdependence of plot and character in plays of this kind. In a recent book on the gradual development of Shakespeare's reputation, Gary Taylor refers to Thomas Rymer as 'the bogeyman of Shakespeare idolatry'.[15] He is a ghost that refuses to be exorcised.

I recognise that what I have produced above is no more than a rationalisation of my dislike for this play, couched in formalistic terms. After all, the reader might object, one could point to structural weaknesses in a play and still like it very much. The previous paragraph might go some way towards explaining why I have pursued that dislike in this particular direction, but it still leaves much unsaid. Let me try to bridge the gap by referring to a previous attempt to treat Rymer's objections, an essay by Nigel Alexander called 'Thomas Rymer and *Othello*' published in 1968.[16] Alexander's basic position is the familiar bardolatrous one that Shakespeare has already anticipated all Rymer's arguments and answered them in the play. Referring to

[15] Gary Taylor, *Reinventing Shakespeare: a Cultural History from the Restoration to the Present* (London, 1989), pp. 33–39, 134–136.
[16] Nigel Alexander, 'Thomas Rymer and *Othello*' (1968), reprinted in *Aspects of 'Othello'* edited by Kenneth Muir and Philip Edwards (Cambridge, 1977), pp. 100–110.

the prejudice that prompts Rymer to find the Othello–Desdemona liaison incredible, Alexander comments that:

> the dramatist has deliberately used this prejudice, expressed by Iago, Brabantio and Roderigo, as part of his play and . . . within the play, he has also provided an answer to it. Desdemona herself answers Rymer's objection:
>
> > My heart's subdued
> > Even to the very quality of my lord.
> > I saw Othello's visage in his mind.
>
> The Duke adopts this answer for himself before the end of the scene.
>
> > And, noble signior,
> > If virtue no delighted beauty lack,
> > Your son-in-law is far more fair than black.[17]

To Alexander, this 'answer' of Shakespeare's is perfectly adequate. If we pay regard to the quality of Othello's *mind*, he is really a white man! Here is the familiar cultural appropriation of skin colour to moral worth. Alexander's comment on Rymer that 'the success of the play in provoking Rymer to expose his own beliefs should warn other critics that the play acts as a mirror up to nature for its audience as well as the characters on stage'[18] could easily be turned back upon him. Here is the point. In *Othello* a successful member of a racial minority struggles hard to win acceptance from his host-community. What Leavis, following G Wilson Knight, calls his 'music' often strikes my ear as an idiom of insecurity, orotund in diction, semantically odd — borrowed robes:

> > 'Tis yet to know —
> > Which, when I know that boasting is an honour,
> > I shall provulgate — I fetch my life and being
> > From men of royal siege, and my demerits
> > May speak, unbonneted, to as proud a fortune
> > As this that I have reached.
>
> > (I.2.19–24)

---

[17] *Aspects of 'Othello'*, pp. 104–105.
[18] *Aspects of 'Othello'*, p. 109.

A man is forced to talk like this to gain acceptance from the Venetian community, an acceptance that he never actually gains, try as he might. His final 'provulgation' and positively last act of service to the Venetian state, his indifferent foster-mother, is to figure himself as a 'malignant and a turbaned Turk', a 'circumcised dog': and in murdering that infidel alter ego, to commit suicide:

> And say, besides, that in Aleppo once
> Where a malignant and a turbaned Turk
> Beat a Venetian and traduced the state,
> I took by th'throat the circumcisèd dog
> And smote him thus.

(V.2.348–352)

This is the ultimate act of annihilative assimilation. And it makes me very uneasy. But that, as they say, is another story.

AFTERTHOUGHTS

1

Do school productions of Shakespeare do more harm than good?

2

Do you agree that Shakespeare should have followed Cinthio in having Iago steal the handkerchief (page 47)?

3

How convinced are you that the 'double calendar' in *Othello* was the result of 'conscious artistry' (page 55) on Shakespeare's part?

4

How helpful do you find it to consider the viewpoints of a range of critics when studying a play?

Mark Thornton Burnett

Mark Thornton Burnett taught at the University of Geneva before taking up his present post as lecturer in English at the Queen's University of Belfast. He has published extensively on Elizabethan and Jacobean drama.

ESSAY

'When you shall these unlucky deeds relate': *Othello* and story-telling

The scene of the grandmother by the fireside, lulling her grand-children to sleep with a tale of fantastic adventures, is one which is familiar to us all. But it is also one which invites us to speculate about the purposes of stories, the reasons for their popularity, their cultural importance. In traditional societies, stories confront anxieties and hopes, and explore sexual or economic difficulties. Through stories, children are helped with the processes of growing up and integrating themselves within the adult community. Perennial issues are addressed, such as achieving independence, establishing origins, finding meaning, negotiating family problems, and fixing a sense of continuity in times of stress and change.[1] With these observations in mind, it would be fair to suggest that stories take into account the

---

[1] See Bruno Bettelheim, *The Uses of Enchantment: The Meaning and Importance of Fairy Tales* (New York, 1977), *passim*.

expectations of the audience; they can be tailored to suit the needs of particular listeners.

What actually constitutes a story is a crucial point. It may be a 'narrative, true or presumed to be true, relating to important events'; a 'narrative of real or, more usually, fictitious events, designed for . . . entertainment'; an autobiography, or, colloquially, a lie.[2] More specialised meanings are implied in the word 'story-teller', which encompasses one 'whose business it is to recite legendary or romantic stories'; a writer of stories, and, again, a liar.[3]

In *Othello*, stories abound and conflict with each other, and the play delineates the attempts of characters to construct narratives for themselves which will permit them to understand personal preoccupations, to replace fear with certainty and self-assurance. Everyone in the drama is suspicious, a prey to rumours, fancy and hearsay, and stories provide a means of confirming or dispelling troubling doubts. Telling can signify knowing and authority (the successful story-teller has access to power), and part of the impact of *Othello* derives from the collision of stories, the struggle for dominance and the explosion of tragic consequences.

At the start we are bombarded with a series of histories of the past which we are obliged to assess. Othello is frequently the subject of these accounts, and differing perceptions of him are expressed before his first appearance. At a bewildering pace, Iago presents us with an impassioned version of recent events and outlines his reasons for hating the Moor. His portrayal of service (I.1.41–66) is a cynical vision of injustice, ruthless exploitation and thwarted opportunities for preferment, but it is impossible to determine what justification lies behind its angry sentiments. However, the military metaphors employed, the stress upon language and the references to appearances introduce prominent concerns and establish at once the story-telling arts that the characters practise.

Quickly shifting the emphasis of his accusations, Iago spins

---

[2] *The Oxford English Dictionary*, edited by J A Simpson and E S C Weiner, 2nd ed., (Oxford, 1989), vol. XVI.
[3] *OED*, vol. XVI.

an elaborate fantasy about Othello's theft of Desdemona, playing upon fears of miscegenation, abduction and rape, and he enlists curt pronouncements, lewd insinuations and gloomy predictions to lend his imaginings urgency and extremity. In response, Brabantio reflects wildly upon Othello's magical powers:

> Judge me the world, if 'tis not gross in sense
> That thou hast practised on her with foul charms,
> Abused her delicate youth with drugs or minerals
> That weakens motion. I'll have't disputed on;
> 'Tis probable, and palpable to thinking:
> I therefore apprehend, and do attach thee
> For an abuser of the world, a practiser
> Of arts inhibited, and out of warrant.

$$\text{(I.2.72–79)}$$

The legal allusions ('Judge', 'disputed' and 'warrant') indicate that Brabantio is anxiously seeking to legitimise his extravagant charges. Similarly, the repetitions and specious logic (he has no concrete evidence) point to worries about the seeming loss of control over his daughter. By lighting upon witchcraft as the method Othello used to gain Desdemona, Brabantio finds for himself a comforting fiction, a story that allows him to cope with the crumbling state of his paternal influence.

Faced with unflattering descriptions of his character, it is not surprising that Othello should retire to the past and celebrate his integrity, prowess and the achievement of military prestige. At salient points through the play, echoes of the sounds of battle are heard, and they stimulate us to revise our ideas about Othello's soldierly activities. While Iago pretends to be distressed by the slight offered to his master, Othello is recollecting the history of his rise to greatness:

> I fetch my life and being
> From men of royal siege, and my demerits
> May speak, unbonneted, to as proud a fortune
> As this that I have reached.

$$\text{(I.2.21–24)}$$

The metaphor 'unbonneted' implies that Othello will proudly declare himself and will not take a position of subservience; while he obeys the state, he refuses to be dominated. As Iago's wiles begin to have an effect, though, Othello is reduced, humbled by suspicions about Desdemona's impurity. Now the battlefield is littered with sexual snares:

> I had been happy if the general camp,
> Pioners and all, had tasted her sweet body,
> So I had nothing known. O, now, for ever
> Farewell the tranquil mind! Farewell content!
> Farewell the plumèd troops and the big wars
> That make ambition virtue — O, farewell!
> Farewell the neighing steed, and the shrill trump,
> The spirit-stirring drum, th'ear-piercing fife,
> The royal banner and all quality,
> Pride, pomp and circumstance of glorious war!
>
> (III.3.342–351)

Indulging in brooding thoughts about Desdemona prostituting herself, Othello unleashes his most violent fantasies. Earlier he spoke reverentially of his royal lineage; now the royal banner is the cause of bitter unhappiness. All the details in the speech bristle with sexual connotations; the trumpet and fife have phallic associations, Othello is pierced, the drum stirs his spirit or progenitive impulses. In this reading of his past, Othello recognises the dawning of a frightening sexuality. As the play progresses, others take over the recounting of Othello's career, as when Lodovico states:

> Is this the noble Moor, whom our full senate
> Call all-in-all sufficient? Is this the nature
> Whom passion could not shake? Whose solid virtue
> The shot of accident nor dart of chance
> Could neither graze nor pierce?
>
> (IV.1.266–270)

Again the language conveys a sense of Othello's resistance to sexual desire: he cannot be shaken, he is solid, and his invulnerability will not be pierced. At the same time, Lodovico's words recall the esteem in which Othello was held and are a timely reminder of a nobility that is struggling to reassert itself.

Although other characters take on story-telling roles in the later stages, for much of the play Othello masterfully manipulates narratives; to the Duke and Senators, he tells of wooing

Desdemona, and his explanation for his conduct reverberates with ironic implications. He relates:

> Of being taken by the insolent foe,
> And sold to slavery; of my redemption thence,
> And portance in my travels' history:
> Wherein of antres vast and deserts idle,
> Rough quarries, rocks, and hills whose heads touch heaven,
> It was my hint to speak — such was the process:
> And of the Cannibals that each other eat,
> The Anthropophagi, and men whose heads
> Do grow beneath their shoulders. This to hear
> Would Desdemona seriously incline
>
> (I.3.136–145)

Othello's story caters to assumptions about his status as a black man even as it seems to resist them: it closely resembles contemporary accounts of travels to newly discovered countries. There is a colonialist dimension to Othello's speech: he sees himself as opposing the 'insolent foe' while he is representative of an ethnic group that was traditionally exploited. While he disparages primitive customs, he himself is a racially oppressed figure in an unfamiliar environment where the attitudes of the white majority prevail.

Whether they be real or imaginary, stories in *Othello* enable characters to communicate a sense of injustice, to banish feelings of insecurity and to counter objections to unconventional conduct in a society used to respecting rigid social norms. By extension, the play also explores the limitations and possibilities of language, and the difficulties in pinning down the 'truth' behind fabrication and fantastic conjecture. These themes emerge in scenes devoted to various forms of reportage. A 'report' is distinguished from a story in that it is a 'formal statement of the results of an investigation', while 'to report' may be defined as to 'say factually' or to 'bring . . . (news).'[4] Juxtaposition is the dramatic procedure adopted in those parts of the drama concerned with the broadcasting of news: the Duke and Senators, for instance, disagree over the number of Turkish galleys bound

---

[4] *OED*, vol. XII.

for Cyprus (I.3), and their argument underscores an awareness of the elusiveness of reliable information and the treacherousness of messages. It parallels, too, Brabantio's relation of the loss of his daughter, property and authority. Likewise, a dialogue takes place between Montano and three gentlemen about Cassio's part in the sea battle (II.1); their favourable comments are in stark contrast to Iago's sardonic, soliloquised opinions in the previous scene. And we anticipate the unravelling of complications and confusion when it becomes clear that a balanced, impartial statement about Desdemona is required; Emilia says towards the end: 'I must needs report the truth' (V.2.129).

Many of the stories that circulate in the play, indeed, centre upon Desdemona and upon irreconcilable views about her nature. A verbal battle is waged between Iago and Cassio as each vies to promote his own version of Desdemona, and their courteous exchange reveals barely concealed mutual hostilities:

CASSIO She is a most exquisite lady.
IAGO And, I'll warrant her, full of game.
CASSIO Indeed, she is a most fresh and delicate creature.
IAGO What an eye she has! Methinks it sounds a parley to provocation.
CASSIO An inviting eye, and yet methinks right modest.
IAGO And when she speaks, is it not an alarum to love?
CASSIO She is indeed perfection.

(II.3.18–25)

In each description in this antiphonal dialogue there may be a grain of 'truth', but neither of the views articulated is granted prominence. To Iago's bawdy remarks, Cassio replies with a dignified reserve, warding off suggestions about Desdemona's sexual availability. Despite Iago's attempts to win over the lieutenant (he even draws upon military terms such as 'alarum' to fuel his argument), Cassio remains unmoved; his idealistic conception of womanhood will not be undermined.

In contrast, Othello quickly succumbs to persuasion, and his story-telling skills are not sufficiently powerful to resist Iago's temptations. Most harrowing for an audience, perhaps, are the central scenes of the play and the spectacle of Othello humiliated by Iago's cunning enticements, made helpless as increasingly outrageous stories entrap him and exacerbate his distress. For their dramatic effect, these scenes depend upon stories, and Desdemona's infidelity is their subject. The devastating fiction of Cassio's dream precipitates Othello into deciding that revenge is his only recourse; Iago states:

> I lay with Cassio lately,
> And being troubled with a raging tooth
> I could not sleep.
> There are a kind of men so loose of soul
> That in their sleeps will mutter their affairs:
> One of this kind is Cassio.
> In sleep I heard him say: 'Sweet Desdemona,
> Let us be wary, let us hide our loves';
> And then, sir, would he gripe and wring my hand,
> Cry 'O sweet creature!' and then kiss me hard,
> As if he plucked up kisses by the roots,
> That grew upon my lips; then laid his leg
> Over my thigh, and sighed and kissed, and then
> Cried 'Cursèd fate that gave thee to the Moor!'
>
> (III.3.410–423)

This is not a homosexual act of love-making, for Iago actually imagines Cassio and Desdemona's physical encounter. Taking the place of the defenceless Desdemona, Iago yields to Cassio's covert advances. Vocabulary is invested with sexual meanings ('lay', 'loose' and 'hard' carry clear erotic messages), and apparently innocuous words allude to the sexual parts ('hand' and 'roots', for example). In addition, as might be expected, the speech concludes with the suggestion that in Cassio's dream the lovers reach a sexual climax; his cries ('Cry', 'sighed' and 'Cried') certainly indicate a passionate, intense experience.

But *Othello* does not only dramatise story-telling through juxtaposition, extended speeches and cut-and-thrust dialogue. Other methods are utilised, and particular words are repeated to deepen the play's investigation of structures of communication, the transference of information and means of self-expression. *Othello* is rife with references to the tongue, the voice, speech, hearing and the ears. 'Go to, charm your tongue' (V.2.182) exclaims Iago, warning Emilia not to disclose the duplicities he has practised. Facilitating either deception or revelation in the drama, the tongue is represented here as an instrument which will bring about recognition of the 'true' state of affairs. The successful command of language guarantees the possession of power, and it is therefore appropriate that the drunken Cassio, newly demoted, should have nothing to say: he complains: 'I cannot speak' (II.3.183). Controlling language may also entail what is not said, and Iago is frustratingly impenetrable when he swears himself to silence — 'From this time forth I never will speak word' (V.2.301) — and refuses to illuminate the mystery of his motivations. As speech is a powerful agent, so is the voice which, in the confusion of *Othello*, becomes a rare reliable form of identification.[5] 'Most reverend signor, do you know my voice?' (I.1.94) asks Roderigo of Brabantio, desperate to be acknowledged. Finally, aural images develop these themes and perform anticipatory tasks. When he reflects upon his daughter's marriage — 'I never yet did hear/ That the bruised heart was piercèd through the ear' (I.3.216–217) — Brabantio ironically looks forward to Iago's infecting stories, to Othello's sexual jealousies, and to the beginnings of his tragic decline.

It is a characteristic of stories that they occupy themselves with beginnings or origins, and raise such questions as family loyalties and obligations, relations with parents, the transition from childhood to adulthood and the quest for autonomy. Mother and father figures take major parts in *Othello*, although their importance may only be implicit and apparent in retrospect. Othello tells Desdemona about the origins of his handkerchief:

> That handkerchief
> Did an Egyptian to my mother give:
> She was a charmer and could almost read
> The thoughts of people. She told her, while she kept it,
> 'Twould make her aimiable and subdue my father
> Entirely to her love; but, if she lost it
> Or made a gift of it, my father's eye
> Should hold her loathèd, and his spirits should hunt
> After new fancies. She, dying, gave it me,

---

[5] One of the subsidiary meanings of 'voice' is 'rumour' (*OED*, vol. XIX), which does not seem to feature in the play.

And bid me, when my fate would have me wive,
To give it her.

(III.4.55–65)

The curious history is alive with warnings intended for the
unsuspecting Desdemona: first, Othello harks back to Brabantio's
fears of the supernatural and casts himself in the image of a
quasi-magician to frighten his wife. Marriage is envisaged by
Othello as an unexciting responsibility and an unattractive
inevitability (the allusion to fate suggests onerous obligations)
so that he can remind Desdemona of her conjugal duties. Even
as he threatens retribution and criticises Desdemona for the loss
of her innocence, however, Othello is sensitive to his own fears
and to the possibility of his being disempowered ('subdue my
father'). Loss is an idea picked up by Desdemona in the willow
song; clearly Othello's predictions have impressed themselves
upon her imagination. She states:

> My mother had a maid called Barbary:
> She was in love: and he she loved proved mad
> And did forsake her. She had a song of willow;
> An old thing 'twas; but it expressed her fortune,
> And she died singing it. That song tonight
> Will not go from my mind: I have much to do
> But to go hang my head all at one side,
> And sing it like poor Barbary — prithee, dispatch.

(IV.3.25–32)

It is as if Desdemona is answering Othello's accusations, for she
also speaks about the death of a parent. Predicting her end, she
goes on to sing of the passing of love, grief and abandonment:
the strains of the supernatural are heard again as Desdemona,
writing her own epitaph, becomes a fortune-teller.

Many of these issues are crystallised in Othello's final speech
in which he looks to the future and expresses anxiety about his
place in posterity:

> Soft you; a word or two before you go.
> I have done the state some service and they know't:
> No more of that. I pray you in your letters
> When you shall these unlucky deeds relate

Speak of me as I am: nothing extenuate,
Nor set down aught in malice. Then must you speak
Of one that loved not wisely, but too well;
Of one, not easily jealous but, being wrought,
Perplexed in the extreme; of one whose hand
Like the base Indian threw a pearl away
Richer than all his tribe; of one whose sùbdued eyes,
Albeit unusèd to the melting mood,
Drop tears as fast as the Arabian trees
Their med'cinable gum. Set you down this:
And say, besides, that in Aleppo once
Where a malignant and a turbaned Turk
Beat a Venetian and traduced the state,
I took by th'throat the circumcisèd dog
And smote him thus.

(V.2.334–352)

It is striking that Othello, having murdered his wife, should now speak only of himself. But the heroic vein of his reflections is apposite and demonstrates a collected response to the conflicts he has undergone. A lofty notion of service preoccupies him; this is not the servile form of employment which Iago condemned. Wanting to be remembered favourably, Othello is insistent that he should be written about: the official sanction of writing is preferable to the untrustworthiness of the spoken word. Nevertheless, inconsistencies and contradictions persist: Othello still tells exotic travel narratives although he needs the 'truth' to be acknowledged; he is a black man who sees himself as a Christian fighting against the infidel. Particularly ambiguous is the close of the story: because he stabs himself, the identity of the 'circumcisèd dog' is unclear, and the equivocal conclusion calls into question the rhetorical utterances upon which Othello's reputation will be founded.

Othello contemplates the treacheries, prevarications and tricks that inform our efforts to communicate. It thematises the slipperiness of language and problems attendant upon storytelling — the distorting effects of the imagination, the difficulty of arriving at an absolute 'truth', the reliability of narratives coloured by personal experience. The play also concerns itself with a distinctive cultural phenomenon, that stories have social functions and are not mere entertainment. We discover in *Othello* some of the reasons for the interest in stories, and characters use them to allay insecurities, to locate sources of stability, and to establish their places in society. This is not always a smooth process, and the contest of the play partly turns upon the question of who becomes the most convincing story-teller. There is a further complication, for *Othello* itself constitutes a story: in its self-consciousness the drama represents one of Shakespeare's most sustained reflections upon his art.

AFTERTHOUGHTS

1

What purposes does Thornton Burnett suggest for story-telling in the opening of this essay? How do these relate to *Othello*?

2

Do you agree that Othello's story (page 65) 'caters to assumptions about his status as a black man even as it seems to resist them'?

3

Do you agree with Thornton Burnett's footnoted suggestion that rumour 'does not seem to feature in the play' (page 68)?

4

Can any narrative ever be 'true'?

Angus Alton

Angus Alton works as a researcher for the University of Oxford Delegacy of Local Examinations. He is also an experienced examiner in English Literature at GCSE and A level.

ESSAY

Why Othello was right to choose Cassio

M R Ridley's Introduction to the Arden edition of *Othello* is in many ways exemplary: it is lucid and so tightly bound to the text that one is often a little uncertain whether particular phrases are direct quotations or exact paraphrases. However, the whole analysis of the play is posited on a claim that seems to me rather dubious. He says:

> *Othello*, to most readers, is not his greatest work, but is his best play, in the narrow sense of 'theatre' probably much his best.
>
> (p. xlv)

And he goes on to describe the plot as 'completely simple, with no sub-plot and no distractions'. In many ways, of course, he is right — there is, technically, no sub-plot — and it is probably true that the temptation scenes work so well on stage that several issues — most notably that of the double time scheme — simply do not arise.

But it seems to me that the structure of the play is full of distractions, many of which make a confident response to the play, whether watched or read, difficult to achieve. Anyone who has taught *Othello* will be familiar with the rather irritated response from students: Why doesn't Othello challenge

Desdemona directly in Act III scene 4? Presumably they also share with me a sense of unease about the equally familiar answers offering generalisations about the nature of jealousy, and Othello's desperately unsettled state of mind. The answers are reasonable enough, but insufficiently persuasive, perhaps because they have little direct grounding in the text.

Emilia also creates a distraction. She is consistently treated badly by her husband, but seems remarkably naïve as to his nature, telling Desdemona and Cassio that Cassio's suit 'grieves my husband/ As if the case were his' (III.3.3–4). More importantly, after giving Iago the handkerchief, or rather after he has snatched it from her, she fears that he wants the handkerchief 'for some purpose of import' (III.3.313). Yet, despite being on stage throughout Act III scene 4 while Othello questions Desdemona about the matter, she says nothing about what she knows, but instead offers rather banal and distracting generalisations about men:

> 'Tis not a year or two shows us a man.
> They are all but stomachs, and we all but food;
> They eat us hungerly, and when they are full,
> They belch us.

(III.4.99–102)

Here, too, the standard explanations of the causes of her failure to speak up — her reluctance to believe Iago has any really evil intentions, and her sense of guilt about her own role in the loss of the napkin — do not quite seem sufficient, although they work as part solutions. What is most significant in terms of the play as 'theatre' is that such explanations tend only to be the province of the reader: the audience is simply aware of the incongruity of the solution to the difficulty being available on stage, but not being provided.

There are, then, already quite good grounds for suspecting Ridley's judgement about the excellence of *Othello* as theatre, as a play which moves undistractedly towards its climax and dénouement. There is an even greater problem than either of those discussed, and it is one which, I believe, also drastically affects our response to the text as readers. It is the problem of Cassio. It is, perhaps, inevitable that, in a play which focuses so closely on a particular pair of characters, many of the rest of the characters should be functional and only half developed. Roderigo certainly fits comfortably into this category, and neither reader nor audience is ever seriously distracted by concern as to why he is so gullible. He exists for three main reasons: as a tool for Iago's dirty work, as a demonstration of Iago's skills, and to allow Iago to reveal much of his thought without Shakespeare having to rely overmuch on soliloquy. All his appearances on stage clearly fulfil one or more of these purposes, and so no real problem occurs.

With Cassio, however, it is rather different. For a start, he is obviously far more important in the plot. Significantly, Roderigo cannot be relied on to carry out any actual actions which Iago incites him to: Iago has to interrupt his pompous attempt to rouse Brabantio in Act I scene 1, and, true to Iago's expectation, he cannot even wound Cassio despite attacking him in the dark. Cassio, on the other hand, has to carry a considerable burden of the plot's credibility and of the play's effectiveness, and this creates an awful lot of problems. I do not think it is possible to resolve them all, but the purpose of this essay is to explore them, and to offer some sort of explanation for at least some of the major ones.

Let me begin by rehearsing some of the difficulties created. Essentially, they boil down to the fact that many aspects of his involvement in the play are indeed functional, and yet, because he is so central to the plot, we expect and in fact require a fuller explanation of why they occur than their function provides. Thus, Cassio has to be cashiered, if Iago's desire to become even with Othello 'wife for wife' (II.1.290) is to be achieved. But the man who, on the first night in Cyprus and while on duty, can be induced into a drunken brawl sits uneasily beside the man who so calmly and authoritatively takes charge during the storm scene. So, too, does the man who keeps, and rather mistreats, a courtesan with one who rather fastidiously apologises for Iago to Desdemona:

> He speaks home, madam; you may relish him more in the soldier than in the scholar

> (II.1.162–163)

and who, even when already slightly drunk, responds to Iago's salacious promptings only with 'An inviting eye, and yet methinks right modest' (II.3.23). More importantly, both these factors, vital though they are for the continuation of Iago's scheme, cast serious doubts over Othello's judgement in appointing Cassio to be his Lieutenant.

Such doubts have two important implications for our understanding of the play. In the first place, taken with the dreadful irony with which Othello tags Iago with the epithet 'honest', it raises questions about Othello's judgement of character in general. Such doubts would tend to place him in the same class of character as Roderigo, and thus considerably affect any sense of the play's status as tragedy. Indeed, given that his trust in Iago can be relatively justified in terms of his own experience, the opinions of others and the skill with which Iago develops his plot (Ridley's Introduction is particularly good on this — pp. lvi–lvii), doubts that arise from elsewhere have particular importance.

The other aspect is more specific, but in many ways even more telling. Much of the tragic impact of Othello depends on the presentation of him in the first half of the play, before Iago's poison has started to act: in it he emerges — it is essential for him to emerge — as a skilled and successful General, calm and competent: a man whom the Venetian state can entrust with the defence of its colonial outposts. If Othello's choice of Lieutenant is mistaken, then what is left of that initial impression with which to withstand the degradations of Iago's plotting? Indeed, as I shall argue later, it is essential for the play's success not only that we, the audience, are convinced that Othello's judgement in this key area is sound, but that we are sure that Iago knows it as well.

Let us begin, however, by unpicking at least some of the knots surrounding Cassio's character in general. It is an important area in that the play develops around Othello's personal misjudgements of the three people who he is closest to, taking the villain to be honest and the innocent to be corrupt. Such wholesale reversal of the truth makes it easy to regard Othello as simply gullible, and in the case of Desdemona his failure to hold on to his perception that 'If she be false, O, then heaven mocks itself!' (III.3.275) is hard to excuse. However, this view fails to do sufficient justice to the skill with which Iago weaves his web. As far as possible, he constructs it from a mixture of half-truth and the workings of Othello's own mind. Twice in his soliloquies he stresses the usefulness of not having to lie, claiming on one occasion 'That Cassio loves her, I do well believe't' (II.1.277) and later he gleefully asks:

> And what's he then that says I play the villain,
> When this advice is free I give, and honest,
> Probal to thinking, *and indeed the course*
> *To win the Moor again?*

(II.3.326–329, my italics)

The view also fails to acknowledge that, in Cassio's case at least, the audience, too, also hardly sees him as blameless. In the case of his drunkenness, there is little that can be said by way of mitigation, save once again to recognise how difficult it is to resist Iago's blandishments. It is useful to remember at this point that it is hard to see how Iago could have gained any ground in his scheming had he not succeeded in this. A sober Cassio would neither have quarrelled with Roderigo, nor have created any noise in dealing with the man, however aggravating. In other words, Cassio's failure at this juncture is the single most important element in the scheme, if for no other reason than that what has happened is incontrovertibly true. Indeed, Iago is in the happy position of being able, as Othello recognises, to 'mince this matter/ Making it light to Cassio' (II.iii.241–242). All that can really be said in Cassio's favour at this point is that he is so full of self-loathing and self-knowledge afterwards:

> It hath pleased the devil drunkenness to give place to the
> devil wrath: one unperfectness shows me another, to make
> me frankly despise myself.

(II.3.287–289)

The question of Bianca is also not an easy one to resolve. For a start, her existence in the play is scarcely necessary. The only strand of the plot to which she contributes significantly is not actually essential, while it strains our credulity to the utmost. The scene when Othello eavesdrops ignominiously on Iago and Cassio in conversation may be a powerful *coup de théâtre*, but it requires not only the extraordinarily selective overhearing by Othello (which, in itself, makes demands on the staging of the scene); it also calls for Cassio to fail to recognise the handkerchief which was Othello's first love token to Desdemona *and* to speak slightingly of a Bianca whom he never actually names. It seems a heavy price to pay for introducing a character who creates such problems for our reading of Michael Cassio.

It is true that Cassio's attitudes to Bianca and to Desdemona are by no means inconceivable. It is a commonplace of feminism that male attitudes to women are inconsistent, requiring a combination of angel and whore as the ideal, but normally settling for classifying all women as one or the other. Once classified, a woman is treated accordingly. Thus, for Cassio, Desdemona is:

> ... a maid
> That paragons description and wild fame;
> One that excels the quirks of blazoning pens,
> And in th'essential vesture of creation
> Does tire the ingener.
>
> (II.1.61–65)

Conversely, Bianca is a mere 'bauble' (IV.1.135) to be treated with utter carelessness. That, at least, is the public image that Cassio must maintain among his brothers in arms; his private treatment of her in Act III scene 4 seems rather more tender, although even here, the moment she appears to imply any grounds for a deeper connection between them, he is quick to attack her:

> Go to, woman!
> Throw your vile guesses in the devil's teeth
> From whence you have them.
>
> (III.4.179–181)

It is worth noting that many of Othello's difficulties also stem from an inability to see Desdemona in other than absolute terms. She is either 'My soul's joy' (II.1.178) or a 'lewd minx' (III.3.472); what is more, to believe one means that the other is really the only plausible alternative view to take. Even the cynical realist Iago takes much the same view: here, though, the angelic option is ruled out, so that all women must be whores. Hence, Iago's casual assumptions about Emilia's sex life. Note, too, how Othello's need to believe that his murder of Desdemona is an act of justice takes the form of arguing that 'she must die, else she'll betray more men' (V.2.6).

Of course, none of this can really excuse Cassio's use of Bianca, but it does, perhaps, partly explain it by giving it context: his behaviour is simply not abnormal in the cultural environment he inhabits, and, more importantly, nor are the attitudes he reveals. Paradoxically, his earlier problems with drink stem from his being persuaded to participate in a 'custom of entertainment' (II.3.32) and show that he is a true member of soldierly company.

The chief question remains: has Othello blundered in choosing Cassio to be his Lieutenant? Certainly, one can imagine a man of weak head and weak will failing a positive vetting procedure; less clearly, keeping a mistress may be seen as dubious in practical as well as moral terms. Thus, the characteristics that Cassio possesses because of the exigencies of the plot tend to work against the view we need to take of him if our response to Othello is to be appropriate for the play's success.

To some extent, of course, our perception of whether Cassio is or is not the right choice for Lieutenant depends on our understanding of what is required of a lieutenant. In this context, the derivation of the word is a helpful place to start: a lieutenant is someone who can take a leader's place in his (or her) absence. Thus, it is necessary for such a person to possess most, if not all, of the same qualities as are required in a leader. At the same time, as a play like *Antony and Cleopatra* points out, it is important not to outdo your leader and become your 'captain's captain' (*Antony and Cleopatra*, III.1.22). The echo of Cassio's description of Desdemona as 'our great Captain's Captain' (II.1.74) is perhaps a warning of things to come: not only is it implicitly dangerous that Othello should allow Desdemona such power, but the focus of the action is Othello's belief that his Lieutenant has supplanted him, not militarily but in his bed.

In terms of leadership qualities, a comparison between the two candidates we are offered, Cassio and Iago, is fairly decisive. True, Iago has intelligence, experience and courage (enough to make us doubtful that 'torments will ope [his] lips' – V.2.303). He shows considerable tactical resource, but crucially it is notoriously difficult to determine what his *strategy* is. It is worth noting that Othello only appoints him Lieutenant at the end of Act III scene 3, when Othello is deeply in Iago's power, when his judgement is already strongly disturbed, and, interestingly, some considerable time after he has relieved Cassio of the office. Is Iago really 'worth no worse a place' (I.1.11)?

Conversely, Cassio is well equipped for the role. He may not be as experienced as Iago, but the speed with which he responds to Roderigo's assault suggests he is a capable fighter. Moreover, despite what is a serious wound, he is essentially in control at the end of the play, even before Lodovico announces it officially. He also takes command easily and naturally while waiting for Othello's storm-tossed ship to arrive, sending gentlemen to find out the identity of each ship as it is spotted (II.1.57 and 95). And it is the ease with which he takes control, without for a moment suggesting that he wishes to supplant Othello — indeed, he keeps everyone's mind focused on his General throughout the anxious wait for his arrival — which make him in many ways an admirable choice as Lieutenant.

Moreover, there are other factors which further strengthen the view that Othello has made the right choice. The first of these derives from a dimension that should never be overlooked: what can be deduced from the attitudes of other characters. Here, significantly, the only voice we hear raised against Othello's choice is that of Iago, and he can hardly be seen as an objective witness. The absence of criticism would prove little, however, were it not for the fact that the Venetian state positively endorses the choice by appointing Cassio as Lord Governor in succession to Othello. The immediate threat may be passed, but it is hard to believe that the appointment would be countenanced unless there was confidence that Cassio would be well capable of dealing with any future emergency. It is worth noting that our only evidence that Cassio has 'never set a squadron in the field' (I.1.22) comes from an Iago embittered at being overlooked.

There are, then, plenty of grounds for the audience to endorse Othello's choice of Lieutenant, as there are for admiring his choice of wife. There remains the issue mentioned above: how far can we feel that Iago knows as well as we do that Othello has made the right decision? For, upon this depends a key element in our reading of the play. Othello may be justified in his choice of wife and Lieutenant; his view of Iago as 'honest' may be seen as entirely reasonable; but, if he should have *known* that Iago was embittered by being overlooked, then his trust in him is a far greater blunder than is otherwise the case.

There is, it must be admitted, one piece of evidence which suggests that Othello should have been more circumspect in the trust he gives to Iago. As so often with the evidence in this play, it comes from Iago's own lips, and is therefore perhaps suspect. Nevertheless, it must be acknowledged that Iago claims to have been actively pursuing the lieutenancy:

> Three great ones of the city,
> In personal suit to make me his Lieutenant,
> Off-capped to him

(I.1.8–10)

The failure of this suit may be a good enough reason for Iago to feel resentful — though hardly on the scale he is — and may make us feel that Othello should have been suspicious of him, but there are more powerful arguments to suggest that Iago is never really persuaded that the decision is a mistaken one.

In the first place, we must assume that Iago is as well aware of the reasons for preferring Cassio outlined above as we are, and as the Venetian government is. After all, if he is as good a soldier as he wants us to believe, he *must* acknowledge the arguments; and if he does not, then he is not such a good soldier, and thus is not 'worth no worse a place' (I.1.11). The Catch-22 is inescapable.

There is, however, a second point which clinches the case, the more so because, once again, it comes from his own lips. In his contempt for Cassio, he describes him as 'a great arithmetician' (I.1.19). The notion is clearly meant to be insulting, and he goes on to complain that Cassio's soldiership is 'Mere prattle without practice' (I.1.26). As a result the term is usually glossed simply as accusing Cassio of having only theoretical knowledge of tactics (the New Penguin, Arden, and Signet editions all offer no more), but the term actually has more importance than this. It must be remembered that Othello is going to Cyprus, an island anticipating invasion and siege. It is notable that, even after the 'mere perdition of the Turkish fleet' (II.2.3), Othello goes to inspect the 'works' going on on the 'fortification'

(III.2.57,59). There is clearly a real need for massive defensive operations on Cyprus, so that any future threat to the island can be more easily dealt with on the spot. Now, building fortifications is no simple matter: it calls for precise calculations of lines of sight, trajectories and, of course, those technical matters inherent in all architecture. One quality that would be useful, if not vital, in a Lieutenant would be the ability to make such calculations: in other words to be a 'great arithmetician'. It is quite likely that Iago prefers open battle to such tactics — or that he would profess to — but it is very unlikely that he is unaware of Cassio's value as Othello's Lieutenant.

None of what I have argued means that we have a play without distractions. Far too many aspects of the plot are too functional to seem convincing developments, and thus our suspension of disbelief is put under considerable strain. Nevertheless, careful consideration of some of these aspects does enable us to see a kind of rationale to them. In particular, we can be assured that Othello's choice of Lieutenant has been a shrewd and informed one. As such, the way a man whose basic judgement of character is so accurate can be so misled becomes the focus of the play, and it is a much more satisfactorily tragic focus than the idea that what goes wrong is just the culmination of a series of blunders by Othello.

AFTERTHOUGHTS

1

How far do you agree that there are essential inconsistencies in Cassio's character, as presented in *Othello*?

2

Do you agree that Bianca's 'existence in the play is scarcely necessary' (page 77)?

3

Does Alton convince you that Othello chose the right person as his Lieutenant?

4

What difference would it make to one's response to the play if one believed that Othello's choice of Lieutenant was misguided?

Peter Cairns

Peter Cairns is Head of English at Dean Close School, Cheltenham, and an experienced A-level examiner.

ESSAY

One that loved too well: a positive view of Othello's love

The tendency of critics has been, in varying degrees, to belittle the stature of *Othello* the play and the heroic tragic image of Othello the man. This has contaminated views of the play, from Rymer's *A Short View of Tragedy* (1693) onwards, and been most contagious since the unsympathetic essays of Eliot and Leavis, published in the thirties and fifties. *Othello* has been presented as of less universal and spiritual significance than later plays, from *King Lear* to *The Tempest*, and the picture of the central character has at times been reduced to that of a braggart or a fool, or both.

At the core of this denigration is the misinterpretation of Othello's love for Desdemona: an unwillingness to believe that a man *can* kill the thing he loves, or even to believe the words in the play itself, which are seen as designedly deceptive. Othello's love, they say, is not love, because it alters when it finds 'alteration'. It is not 'an ever fixèd mark'. These words from Sonnet 116 may remind us of France's wooing of Cordelia in *King Lear*. Othello's love does not seem to be consistent like that of Desdemona or Cordelia, or of Romeo or Troilus, or of the later heroines, from Imogen in *Cymbeline* to Miranda in *The Tempest*.

Scepticism on this matter is often due to realistic and domestic modes of plot, dialogue, motives and relationships which seem to dominate much of the play. 'Nowadays', wrote Jane Adamson in *Othello as Tragedy* (1980), 'it is commonly agreed that *Othello* lends itself best to naturalistic interpretations'. *Othello* is seen to operate at one restricted imaginative level. The realistic detail in the play; the unusual amount of information we are given about Venice, its empire, government and society; insights into the fears and desires of so many characters, conveyed in the most commonplace and immediate forms of prosaic gossip and rumour — all of these factors create a wood-for-trees syndrome which causes us to shy away from grander meaning and to focus too narrowly on negative aspects. We are lured towards a negative interpretation of all that happens: to share the vision of Iago. Too often he is the star of stage performances and in the mind of the reader. We are as disinclined as Iago to believe in heroic absolute values. Love is readily seen as a 'lust of the blood' and a 'permission of the will' (I.3.331–332). We forget that cynicism is an essential element of evil as Shakespeare portrays it, and that his cynics, from Thersites in *Troilus and Cressida* to Antonio in *The Tempest*, have nothing to recommend them.

If Othello's love is not admirable, he is no hero and the play is no tragedy. However, a positive response to the love relationship, to the presentation of Desdemona's extraordinary goodness, and to the words which express Othello's own feelings about her must point towards both heroic idealism and tragic waste; and a glance at Shakespeare's source should encourage us to look in this direction.

In Shakespeare's source-book, which he must have read in French or Italian, he found this picture of the lovers:

> It happened that a virtuous lady of marvellous beauty, named Disdemona, fell in love with the Moor, moved thereto by his valour; and he, vanquished by the beauty and the noble character of Disdemona, returned her love; and their affection was so mutual that although the parents of the lady strove all they could to induce her to take another husband, she consented to marry the Moor; and they lived in such harmony and peace in

Venice that no word ever passed between them that was not
affectionate and kind.

(Cinthio, Hecatommithi, trans. J E Taylor (1855), III, 7)

The study of the alteration of source material is the most
important means of discovering the dramatist's intentions. He
changed much from Cinthio's story. He took away, for example,
Iago's child, Cassio's wife, Iago's hatred and murder of Desdemona, and many tortures. He added, for example, Roderigo,
Turks, a sea-storm and a drinking scene. The purpose again and
again is to achieve greater dramatic concision and intensity. On
the other hand, Cinthio's simple account of Othello's love seems
to have been accepted uncritically. Just two important changes
are strikingly noticeable in Shakespeare's story. Cinthio places
Desdemona's plea to go with her husband to Cyprus in the
private context of their own dining-room. She does not stand
before the whole Senate to insist upon the 'rites of love'. This
boldness in Shakespeare's version must shock her father unbear-
ably — it will drive him to his death — and it may even surprise
Othello himself as he discovers the wondrous relationship he has
embarked upon. This first detail therefore provides material for
the naturalistic approach: Shakespeare is concerned with
psychological features which affect the central relationship. This
moment will be returned to later.

The second detail is interesting at a higher level. In Cinthio
there are no voices from beyond death: no Roderigo echoing
Iago's name 'after long seeming dead'; nor the infinitely more
moving voice of Desdemona concerned, Christ-like, only to
redeem the murderer's guilt:

EMILIA   O, who hath done this deed?
DESDEMONA   Nobody — I myself — farewell,
Commend me to my kind lord — O, farewell!

(V.2.124–126)

Critics are, it seems, embarrassed by these words. The
Signet editor calls them 'unbelievable'; yet they show us what
Shakespeare made of the phrase 'the beauty and noble character
of Disdemona'. This is what Othello valued more than a 'world/
Of one entire and perfect chrysolite' (V.2.143–144); this mira-
culous love is where he hoped to have 'garnered up [his] heart'
(IV.2.56).

Such passages should encourage us towards grander interpretations and more positive attitudes than those influenced by Eliot or Leavis. *Othello*, in spite of its realism, is as full of symbolic patterns and structures as any of the great tragedies. We can hardly ignore the semiotic force of black and white, whether in simple visual contrast, or in the perversion of values, or in the intriguingly named Bianca. Neither can we ignore the repeated reference to heaven and hell, angels and blacker devils, and to the balancing of characters in so many areas, and the journey through the storm which takes the hero to a different, even opposite, self. As in a Morality play, Desdemona and Iago represent extremes of good and bad, or selflessness and selfishness. Othello, having been entranced by the one, is in the briefest space of time ensnared soul and body by the other. However, he is surely not an Everyman-figure like Lear, poised because of his ordinary humanity between the two extremes, nor does he share the moral mediocrity of Macbeth. Othello is an extreme character — an idealist if ever there was one — described by Cinthio as 'very valiant and of great skill and prudence', but more strikingly by Iago as 'of a constant loving and noble nature'. He is, as Cinthio puts it, 'vanquished by the beauty and the noble character of [Desdemona]'. First and last, what amazed Othello was Desdemona's *giving* of pity, of grace and love. Hers were the first outrageous moves in the courtship — in spite of every convention of family and society, hers were the risks:

> She gave me for my pains a world of sighs:
> . . .
> And bade me, if I had a friend that loved her,
> I should but teach him how to tell my story,
> And that would woo her.

> (I.3.158–165)

This loving surrender of self, so generous and brave, so entirely alien to his forty years' experience of the big wars, dazzled Othello. Like Cordelia's love, it redeemed nature from the general curse and from the ways of desire; and rather like Lear, Othello wanted it at the centre of a new world, where the two lovers would sing like birds in a cage, independent of, and superior to, the world he had previously occupied. There is even something of Lear's defiance of the world in Othello's impetuous response to his discovery. He has immediately 'ta'en away this old man's daughter' (I.3.78) and married her. Because his love is for an epitome of virtue, he sees no fault in the downright violence of the act, and is convinced that his perfect soul will manifest itself to everyone's satisfaction. Brabantio's jewel becomes more precious than a world made of topaz or a 'pearl . . . / Richer than all his tribe' (V.2.343–344). He felt like Donne's lover in 'The Sunne Rising':

> She is all states and all princes I;
> Nothing else is.

The preciousness of his possession is of course so dazzling that Othello is blinded: to the enormity of his elopement, to the common humanity of his wife, to the power of his own sexual desire, and to the evil in the world hidden behind the honest image of his ensign.

His own love involves a matching abandonment to gratitude and admiration far greater than his public account of it:

> She loved me for the dangers I had passed,
> And I loved her, that she did pity them.
>
> (I.3.166–167)

and an almost matching surrender of a key part of his identity:

> But that I love the gentle Desdemona
> I would not my unhousèd free condition
> Put into circumscription and confine
> For the seas' worth.
>
> (I.2.25–28)

Othello is presented as a professional soldier, perhaps in his late forties, totally self-assured and self-contained, who has found a thing of such value that his previous confident estimate of his life has to be reassessed.

So this apparently perfect love in Desdemona inspires a love at least as powerful in Othello. Iago admits:

> The Moor — howbeit that I endure him not —
> Is of a constant, loving, noble nature,
> And, I dare think, he'll prove to Desdemona

> A most dear husband.
>
> (II.1.279–282)

Given time, the relationship would be not only wonderful, but also secure. There are signs in Act II, before Iago's first move, not only of the strain of newness, as in the 'bachelor' cry:

> . . . I do beseech thee, grant me this;
> To leave me but a little to myself
>
> (III.3.84–85)

but also, as John Bayley suggests in his book *The Characters of Love* (1960), of adjustment and compromise in the speeches which follow.

Wonder is the most powerful element in Othello's emotions at the start: the delighted discovery of the uniqueness of the loved one, balanced by an amazed gratitude for a new sense of his own worth. There is no time yet for any profound acquaintance with the beloved, but there are other factors in the relationship which, because of its newness, make it vulnerable. One of these is the concept of possession, a richly ambiguous word in the context of this play.

Emilia reminds us of an accepted view of woman's status in marriage — 'I nothing, but to please his fantasy' (III.3.296), and 'They are all but stomachs, and we all but food' (III.4.100) — the wife is a possession to have and to hold. Brabantio cries to Roderigo 'O would you had had her' (I.1.176). For Othello, the revelation of Desdemona's worth and beauty makes her infinitely covetable. She must be his, although he knows he must be 'free and bounteous to her mind' (I.3.262). Much of his later pain comes from being cheated of his possession:

> O, curse of marriage!
> That we can call these delicate creatures ours
> And not their appetites! I had rather be a toad
> . . .
> Than keep a corner in the thing I love
> For others' uses.
>
> (III.3.265–270)

This attitude, which is of course only a part of his original feeling — as it is part of any physical relationship — is encouraged by Iago. The idea of 'having' becomes 'tast[ing] her sweet body' (III.3.343) and satisfaction of the appetite. Also, he is urged to see his ownership of her as being as straightforward a matter as her ownership of a handkerchief.

The one outstanding use of the word 'possession' in the last Act of the play shows the dreadful change which has affected his original response to her: 'Whip me, ye devils,/ From the possession of this heavenly sight!' (V.2.275–276). Growing out of the simple meaning are grotesque ideas of being possessed by a devil and being perversely obsessed by this image of heavenly beauty.

The instinct 'to have and to hold' is a legitimate part of married love, but it is a difficult feeling to cope with because it is connected to that other element, sexual possession. Many have noticed that in the first two Acts, Othello never mentions any sexual aspect of the relationship, whereas by Act IV he talks of little else. Many have wondered if his account of purely Platonic love through pity might be disingenuous: a politic line to take before a jury, as it were, from Alabama. Again, such scepticism is easy but unnecessary and unhelpful. The account is incomplete, but it does show the pure centre. The extra element of sexual union had only just been revealed to Othello. His delight can be felt in the meeting in Cyprus: it is expressed in that remarkable musical flood of poetry. It may however be touched by puzzlement.

His impression of beauteous virtue in Desdemona presumably involves the difficult Christian concept of chastity. The word comprehends a range of attitudes from a pragmatic self-control to a profound disgust or shame about sexual desire and activity. Othello finds no shame. His understanding of her chastity must include her generosity, immediacy and frankness; he must come to terms with the 'violence' of the elopement and her public appeal to be allowed to sleep with him — the detail which Shakespeare added to Cinthio's story. Whatever his own sexual experience, he may be in some degree surprised at his young bride's delight in love-making, an area of uncertainty which Iago will explore with relish. His own aching sense of her desirability only rarely gleams from the text, although the actor must show it on stage throughout the play. It is most clear in the scene where he kills her. As he had feared, her 'body and beauty' almost 'unprovide' his mind (IV.1.204): beauty shining like a flame, the skin whiter than snow, smoother than alabaster, the balmy breath like the scent of a rose which he must smell on the tree before he plucks it. Of course, under pressure from Iago, obsessed images of copulation become more widespread in Othello's speech, but as is appropriate these have the impersonality of pornography: disembodied physical features, noses, ears and lips; rutting animals, goats and monkeys.

Othello's love is not simply an amalgam of self-love and lust. It is composed of a variety of emotions and instincts, none of which is essentially ignoble — least of all desire and self-esteem. It is heroic because of its idealism and intensity — he loves too well — it is tragic because of its lack of worldly wisdom. Near the end of the play, where he realises what he has lost, it is easy to see the real nature of his love, the value of Desdemona's uniqueness to him. The pearl and chrysolite images show that he had been presented with a new and perfect world. Any qualifying detail or doubt would so have annulled that perfection that chaos would come again, the bliss destroyed. That is why he has been so perversely uninterested in cross-examination. Nothing could restore the pristine splendour of his possession: the theft is irreparable. This is the tragic result of seeing the world in black and white.

Nevertheless, Othello's image of Desdemona is not of an angel or an ideal. She is a distinct individual with a beguiling variety of facets, talents and charms. She 'loves company,/ Is free of speech, sings, plays, and dances well' (III.3.182–183); she is 'delicate with her needle', 'will sing the savageness out of a bear', and is 'Of . . . high and plenteous wit and invention' (IV.1.186–189). When he describes at length what her loss means to him, in Act IV, there is no reason to disbelieve him:

> Had it pleased heaven
> To try me with affliction, had they rained
> All kinds of sores and shames on my bare head,
> Steeped me in poverty to the very lips,
> Given to captivity me and my utmost hopes,
> I should have found in some place of my soul
> A drop of patience. But, alas, to make me
> A fixèd figure for the time of scorn
> To point his slow unmoving finger at!

Yet could I bear that too, well, very well:
But there where I have garnered up my heart,
Where either I must live, or bear no life,
The fountain from the which my current runs,
Or else dries up — to be discarded thence
Or keep it as a cistern for foul toads
To knot and gender in! Turn thy complexion there,
Patience, thou young and rose-lipped cherubin,
Ay, there look grim as hell!

(IV.2.46–63)

This speech is like a loose extended sonnet of tortured love.
It surely contains the answers for anyone who chooses to be
cynical about Othello. For nine lines he lists physical and
psychological horrors, hells of disease and disgrace which might
have brought him to despair. The rhythms of the early lines,
driven on by a torrent of punishing verbs, prove that these are
not just rhetorical exercises in hypothesis: that Job's sufferings
are imagined as his own, as if sores, shames, poverty and
captivity had consumed his life. The first 'But' is significantly
placed. Othello acknowledges the essential importance of his
self-esteem as he feels himself sharing Job's humiliation:

But now they that are younger than I have me in derision . . .
And now am I their song, yea, I am their byword.

(Job 30:1, 9)

Shakespeare's concise image makes the shame eternal: the
cuckold will remain the fashionable butt of pointing and laughter
for as long as the sun shines on a sun-dial. But this is not the
core of Othello's pain. He rejects this view of his soul emphati-
cally:

Yet I could bear that too, well, very well

(IV.2.55)

The climactic 'But' in the eleventh line marks the change
from worldly to spiritual, selfish to selfless considerations, which
shows us the real meaning and value of his love. His love for
Desdemona is described as an area where he has 'garnered up'
(IV.2.56) his heart. The word conveys the storing of precious
grain for the winter months, a means of life which will last

beyond present preoccupations, perhaps beyond death. The image here and that of the fountain two lines later are the language of the religious convert. Desdemona's love has changed his concept of himself in relation to his life, so that it is now all he wants to live for: a source of strength ('garnered') and inspiration ('fountain'); nothing to do with pride or possession. To imagine its loss is to imagine desecration — a holy shrine reduced to 'a cistern for foul toads/ To knot and gender in', or abattoir where flies swarm over rotting meat.

We may have been surprised at the extravagance of earlier pictures of Desdemona, 'a maid/ That paragons description and wild fame' who 'in th'essential vesture of creation/ Does tire the ingener' (II.1.61–65). Desdemona may be 'divine' Desdemona (II.1.73) but that does not mean that she is a goddess, as can easily be shown; rather the adjective stresses that her physical beauty is matched by extraordinary spiritual qualities, in particular an amazing capacity for selfless love and self-denial.

> Let nobody blame him; his scorn I approve

> (IV.3.49)

Her song anticipates her final words. This is what Othello's soul has responded to: he has been as amazed as we are.

Amazed, delighted, and bewildered, because not only does his soul respond, but also his 'sense aches' (IV.2.67–68) at her, even though she deceived her father and has sweaty palms and is capable of nagging. He is bewildered because things happen so fast that he has not learned that she cannot say 'whore', nor can she even understand Emilia's pragmatic views on adultery:

> I do not think there is any such woman.

> (IV.3.82)

Othello loves not wisely, but too well. A bright image of perfect love changes his life. An evil man distorts and obscures that vision and the lover is led from a world of light to chaos and darkest hell. He believes that if his image is capable of question, infection or qualification, it cannot have been perfect. He is numbed and blinded by the loss.

By the end, he knows that the love has been real and that he will never see it again. Desdemona, like Cordelia, offers a love like that of Christ, forgiving and redemptive; but Othello's soldierly sense of justice makes him reject any hope of redemption. In the Catholic context of the play, his suicide must mean that he condemns himself to eternal death. Our only consolation is that in a world where Iago and the tribe of hell bustle so effectively under a marble heaven, a world which reflects so convincingly the image of our real world, the love of Desdemona and of Othello, although pitiably fragile, could, for a while, exist.

AFTERTHOUGHTS

1

Do you think that real love ought to be unalterable?

2

Do you agree that 'If Othello's love is not admirable, he is no hero and the play is no tragedy' (page 85)?

3

Do you agree that Macbeth is guilty of 'moral mediocrity' (page 87)?

4

Does Cairns convince you that Othello loved 'too well' (page 93)?

Claire Saunders

Claire Saunders teaches English at Lavant House, Chichester. She is an experienced A-level examiner.

ESSAY

The Willow scene

Scenes honoured by nicknames tend to present obviously dramatic events or situations — the 'Sleepwalking scene' in *Macbeth*, the 'Courtroom scene' in *The Merchant of Venice*, the 'Ghost scene' in *Hamlet*. In *Othello* we can identify a 'Storm scene' (II.1), a 'Drinking scene' (II.3), a 'Temptation scene' (III.3) and a 'Murder scene' (V.2). But what of the so-called 'Willow scene' (IV.3)? In contrast to the others it seems minor and marginal: no one kills or gets killed; no one so much as argues; nothing is revealed or discovered — in fact the scene contributes nothing at all to the plot. What then is so special about the 'Willow scene', and why is a production of *Othello* without it inconceivable? Within a play set mainly in a military garrison, concerning male achievements and ideas, male ambitions and male frustrations, this scene, with its specifically female substance and tone, not only defines the female response to the male concerns of the play but also serves to focus and intensify the male tragedy.

Although the Willow scene is probably thought of as an intimate 'two-hander', a short dialogue between two women as Emilia helps Desdemona to prepare for bed, it is ushered in by eight lines of a very different character, lines which are crucial to what follows:

LODOVICO   I do beseech you, sir, trouble yourself no further.

OTHELLO   O, pardon me: 'twill do me good to walk.

LODOVICO   Madam, good night. I humbly thank your ladyship.

DESDEMONA   Your honour is most welcome.

OTHELLO   Will you walk, sir?
 O, Desdemona!

DESDEMONA   My lord?

OTHELLO   Get you to bed on th'instant. I will be returned
forthwith. Dismiss your attendant there. Look't be done.

(IV.3.1–8)

The style of Lodovico's leave-taking is apparently conventional
— the kind of exchange that might take place at any front door
after a formal dinner party — but the text is taut with unspoken
significance derived from the preceding episode (IV.1), in which
Othello's private passions had burst into public shame. After the
display of Desdemona's being summoned, dimissed, re-summoned
(implicating the bewildered Lodovico) and finally re-dismissed,
Lodovico must now be anxious to escape from the host who has
caused him so much embarrassment. His 'trouble yourself no
further' rings almost comically in its polite euphemism, as he
tries to avoid Othello's insistence on accompanying him. But his
farewell to Desdemona is sober and we are aware, behind the
stock phrases, that he takes with him the image of her being
humiliated and struck by her husband — 'this would not be
believed in Venice.' (IV.1.242). The audience's sense that
Lodovico represents Venice and has identified himself as a
support for Desdemona, makes his departure here seem like a
desertion: he has embodied the ordered, civilised code which
bred and still cherishes Desdemona, but now she is cut off from
that life-line.

 So Othello's parting words sound menacingly. The 'Get you
to bed' and 'I will be returned' are bland enough, but the
'Dismiss your attendant' together with the repetitive 'on
th'instant' and 'forthwith' and the insistent 'Look't be done'
make for a sinister effect. The audience, of course, has good
reason to fear Othello's conjunction of 'Get you to bed' and 'I will
be returned' since we have witnessed the plan, made by Iago and
Othello: Desdemona is to be strangled in her bed and it is to be
done 'this night' (IV.1.203). On this baleful note the men and
their attendants depart and the stage is left to the two women.

The women's dialogue starts somewhat constrainedly. Their previous private exchange was in the aftermath of Othello's crude and abusive charade (IV.2), when Emilia had been cast as bawd to Desdemona's whore. Emilia's introductory 'How goes it now?' (IV.3.10) echoes her 'How do you, madam?' (IV.2.95) of the earlier scene. Then Desdemona had been dazed and dry-eyed; here again she eschews the stereotyped female response of weeping. Emilia's 'he looks gentler than he did' (line 10) is not just a reminder to us that she has not shared Desdemona's experience of Othello's parting words (though to us, who have, the reassurance rings ironically); it is also Emilia's way of urging Desdemona to confide in her. But Desdemona remains stoical, or perhaps stunned, merely paraphrasing Othello's instructions (lines 7–8). In fact it is almost direct repetition, rather than paraphrase:

> He says he will return incontinent.
> He hath commanded me to go to bed,
> And bade me to dismiss you.
>
> (lines 11–13)

Although Desdemona's substituted 'incontinent' does have connotations of rage and madness (which we are likely to feed into the accumulating sense of menace), it does not necessarily denote anything more than Othello's 'forthwith', and Desdemona's dutiful reporting of her husband's words both underlines, for the audience, the note of doom and presents Desdemona almost as an automaton programmed for her own destruction.

> Give me my nightly wearing, and adieu.
> We must not now displease him.
>
> (lines 15–16)

Against this restrained docility the audience gain an emotional release from Emilia's outburst — 'I would you had never seen him' (line 17). It also serves to break the constraint between the two women and move the dialogue into a different mode.

The second phase of the women's scene is immediately, understandably, focused on carrying out Othello's instructions: Desdemona methodically, but with an undercurrent of urgency, prepares for bed. In counterpoint to the mechanical obedience of her actions there now runs a spontaneous sequence of emotional reflections, unleashed by the challenge of Emilia's 'I would you had never seen him'. In this episode Desdemona's actions consist, precisely, in obeying Othello's words, but her words now start to weave in and out of the implications of his actions. Through her actions and her words — what the audience see and what they hear — the unique pathos of the figure of Desdemona is experienced.

The actions (actually carried out by Emilia, Desdemona remaining physically passive) are defined by a series of stage directions naturalistically incorporated into Desdemona's speech: 'Prithee, unpin me . . . No, unpin me here . . . Lay by these . . . get thee gone' (lines 20–55). Since Emilia does not go out to fetch the suggested nightgown (line 33), we can assume that what the audience see is the systematic undressing of Desdemona (and, probably, the loosening of her hair), until she is left, presumably, in the conventional undergarment of the time, a simple white shift. This sequence of actions serves two main purposes — to focus our imaginations and to pace the accompanying dialogue.

The symbolism of Desdemona's disrobing for bed is both powerful and complex. Firstly, Desdemona is changed from the formally decked figure of the General's wife to the informal one of a simple woman. In fact by the end of the process the woman has become almost a child, investing Emilia with a sort of 'Nurse' role as Desdemona questions and clings, increasingly emphasising her own naïvety. Being 'stripped of her garments' imparts a sense of vulnerability (the reverse is seen at the end of *Antony and Cleopatra*, when Cleopatra calls for her robes, to be decked out for her triumphant encounter with Death). Desdemona is destined not to triumph but to be sacrificed; she is going to her death-bed. The bed is part of the 'poetic justice' of Othello's plan — 'even the bed she hath contaminated', as Iago put it (IV.1.206–207). The death-bed is also, therefore, the wedding-bed, and to Desdemona it represents a hoped-for magical solution. After the scene in which she had been abused as a whore, her apparently illogical request to Emilia to 'Lay on my bed my wedding sheets' (IV.2.104) must have expressed her subconscious desire to get back to the purity and joy of her wedding night. Emilia has clearly decoded the request so that now, as Desdemona is preparing to dismiss her, Emilia announces, as a form of comforting reassurance, 'I have laid those sheets, you bade me, on the bed' (line 21). Desdemona responds to the mention of the sheets with an instinctive fancy:

> If I do die before thee, prithee shroud me
> In one of those same sheets.

(IV.3.23–24)

Although she seems to dismiss the fancy in self-mockery ('how foolish are our minds!', line 22), it is heavily ironic for the audience. The wedding sheets do literally, as well as symbolically, become Desdemona's shroud, herself, 'Pale as [her] smock' (V.2.271), the chaste sacrifice.

Despite its ritual and symbolic dimension, however, the disrobing of Desdemona is also relaxed and naturalistic. The basically domestic, intimate nature of the actions is emphasised by the accompanying dialogue. The conversation is unforced, Desdemona — who dominates it at this stage — ranging fluently, but apparently aimlessly, from one topic to another: a glowing declaration of love for her husband ('my love doth so approve him/ That even his stubbornness, his checks his frowns — / . . . have grace and favour in them' (lines 18–20); an apparently random reference to death and wedding sheets (lines 23–24); the casual recall of the dinner guest ('This Lodovico is a proper man', line 34); the almost involuntary song of 'willow' which persists through thirty lines of the scene (lines 25–54). It is a 'stream of consciousness' sequence, following the logic of emotion and intuition rather than reason. But of course there is a controlling dramatic logic, in that Desdemona is responding all the time to Othello's frightening behaviour; this essentially male form of irrationality is the unspoken but dominating influence.

The vulnerability of Desdemona's situation and her perception of it make pathos the keynote of the episode. The pathos is gathered up and expressed in the song. The 'willow song' is traditional in both words and tune — the haunting lute melody associated with a lamenting 'willow garland' refrain was well established before the anonymous ballad 'A Lover's Complaint' was published. Desdemona avoids sentimentality — which would make true pathos impossible — by keeping the song at two or three removes from herself: she emphasises its dated quality — 'An old thing 'twas' (line 28); she associates it with a distant figure — 'My mother had a maid called Barbary' (line 25); she introduces it with an engaging inconsequentiality and self-deprecating humour:

> That song tonight
> Will not go from my mind: I have much to do,
> But to go hang my head all at one side,
> And sing it like poor Barbary
>
> (lines 29–32)

But of course the song is heart-rending in both content and delivery. There is the central figure of a deserted woman (though in the original 'Complaint' the 'poor soul' was masculine), her desolate pose, the pathetic fallacy of the streams which 'murmured her moans' (line 42) and the tears which 'softened the stones' (line 44), and the final callous dismissal, 'If I court moe women, you'll couch with moe men' (line 54). Then there is also the framing story of Barbary — 'he she loved proved mad/ And did forsake her' (lines 26–27), and 'she died singing it' (line 29). And Shakespeare's audience must also have been haunted by echoes from his recent *Hamlet*, where the deserted and distracted Ophelia had fallen from a willow tree and drowned, 'Which time she chanted snatches of old songs' (*Hamlet* IV.4.176). It is all encapsulated in the image of the willow, always in Shakespeare — and possibly throughout Elizabethan drama — inseparable from its emblematic function as a symbol of forsaken or betrayed love. Here, reinforced by the falling cadence of the song's refrain ('Sing all a green willow' . . . 'Sing willow, willow, willow' . . . 'Sing all a green willow must be my garland'), the willow has come to be synonymous with a whole scene centred on doomed love.

In addition Shakespeare adapts the song for further dramatic effects. Firstly it is frighteningly interrupted by Desdemona's 'Hark, who is't that knocks?' (line 50); Emilia seeks to banish the alarm with 'It's the wind' (line 51) but coming, as it does, just after the fearful sense of urgency in Desdemona's 'Prithee hie thee; he'll come anon' (line 47), the alarm remains, adding poignancy to Desdemona's determined return to her song. (Anyone who has seen Orson Welles's film will remember the terrifying effect of the knocking, wailing wind in this scene.) Secondly, the song goes interestingly astray, with Desdemona having to correct herself with a 'Nay, that's not next' (line 50). The interesting thing is that the line she thus dismisses — 'Let nobody blame him; his scorn I approve' (line 49) — reasserts itself at the end of the play: before dying, Desdemona regains consciousness and her final words, in answer to Emilia's 'O, who hath done this deed?' are 'Nobody — I myself — farewell./ Commend me to my kind lord — O, farewell!' (V.2.124–126). So the line in the song that she rejects actually expresses that self-denigrating, accepting quality that is so characteristic of Desdemona, and so fatal. Thirdly, the last verse of the song is not in the original 'Complaint' and is introduced by Shakespeare to move the whole scene into another mode:

> I called my love false love, but what said he then?
> . . .
> If I court moe women, you'll couch with moe men.
>
> (lines 52–54)

The unjust imputations here, and the tone of protest, tie the song firmly into Desdemona's own story (adding to the obvious parallels between herself and the 'poor soul' and 'poor Barbary'). When, in the earlier scene (IV.2), Desdemona was 'bewhored' by her husband she responded with dazed incomprehension:

> I cannot say 'whore':
> It does abhor me now I speak the word;
> To do the act that might the addition earn
> Not the world's mass of vanity could make me.
>
> (IV.2.160–163)

Now, however, as her song ends, Desdemona returns to Othello's charge and embarks on a deliberate, probing dialogue with Emilia.

The topic of women's chastity serves to polarise Desdemona and Emilia. Desdemona catechises Emilia, her series of questions, followed by exclamations of disbelief, establishing her as an abstract of female virtue — almost a figure from a Morality play. In the dialogue Emilia is thus cast, superficially, as an opposite stereotype — Worldly Lusting as opposed to Chaste Loving, perhaps. Desdemona's speeches have an almost irritatingly child-like style, though her solemnly reiterated total rejection of the very concept of unfaithfulness gives her character a noble simplicity. In contrast Emilia emerges as complex, witty and mature — and this, of course, is what Shakespeare needed to establish before his final scene.

Emilia dominates the final section of the Willow scene. Pushed into a corner by Desdemona's naïve incredulity, she turns and delivers a powerful 'credo'. Her speech (lines 83–102) is a brilliant counterbalance to the 'willow song', in content, style and viewpoint; instead of lyrical lament there is sharp polemic. It is a marvellous antidote to the 'hapless female victim' icon. Instead of championing female chastity and innocence, Emilia takes on men at their own level, accepting the charges but then countering them:

> But I do think it is their husbands' faults
> If wives do fall.

(lines 85–86)

There is a refreshing element of the Wife of Bath in Emilia (as, perhaps, there is of that opposite *Canterbury Tales* figure, Patient Griselda (of *The Clerk's Tale*), in Desdemona). A strong sexual thread runs through Emilia's argument as she talks of husbands who 'slack their duties,/ And pour our treasures into foreign laps' (lines 86–87), in her references to 'sport' (lines 96,100) and in her claim for equality:

> Let husbands know
> Their wives have sense like them: they see and smell,
> And have their palates both for sweet and sour
> As husbands have.

(lines 92–95)

But Emilia is not presented as immoral — quite the contrary. Her speech restores to women the frank and wholesome outlook which was originally displayed in Desdemona's insistence on accompanying her husband to Cyprus, so as not to miss 'The rites for which I love him' (I.3.254). Emilia's major role in the play will be as the voice of truth and moral clarity when it will be she who reveals, defines and denounces the crimes of both Othello and Iago. Here, at the end of the Willow scene she moves from 'minor' into 'major' character. The stridency of her tone is perhaps necessary for her dramatic role and is welcome as a counter to the almost soggy sweetness of Desdemona's naïve idealism. But Emilia will die lyrically, singing snatches of the 'willow song' (V.2.246) — a poignant irony.

Having reached the end of the Willow scene all seems set for the tragic finale: the heroine, ready and prepared as sacrificial victim awaits the executioner. Why doesn't Shakespeare move straight into the death-bed scene, instead of interposing the attack on Cassio and murder of Roderigo, which could have been dealt with earlier? Two great versions of the text — Welles's film and Verdi's opera — do just that and achieve powerfully dramatic finales. But I think Shakespeare is more subtle. By separating the Willow scene and Desdemona's death he enables his final scene to rise above pathos. Without the continuity from the 'disrobing' scene, Desdemona is just a figure asleep in bed, so that, instead of seeing Othello in simple melodramatic terms as the advancing shadow of villainy, we can concentrate on his tragic conflict. When Othello enters with 'It is the cause, it is the cause, my soul' (V.2.1), the focus is entirely on him; Desdemona has taken her proper dramatic position as the subject and object of Othello's tragedy.

So the Willow scene has served its purpose. Despite contributing nothing to the plot and totalling little more than 100 lines, each section — from Othello's departure, through Desdemona's reflective undressing and the song, and on to the dialogue on chastity and Emilia's challenge to men — can, in itself, be seen to contribute crucially to the whole. The themes of innocence and sexuality have been explored, giving depth to the concluding tableau in which Desdemona will lie shrouded in her wedding sheets; the character of Emilia has been developed with a view to her subsequent role; above all the strong pathos inherent in the figure of Desdemona has been explored and exorcised. But the sections also work together to make a scene that is uniquely female in both structure and style; despite the sinister circumstances, the women's dialogue, relaxed in its ebb and flow, seems a moment of tranquillity caught between the frenzy past and the violence to come.

AFTERTHOUGHTS

1

Can you suggest any other name for the 'Willow scene'?

2

Do you find yourself at all irritated by Desdemona's 'child-like' simplicity in this scene (page 102)?

3

Do you agree that the Willow scene marks Emilia's transition to 'major' character (page 103)?

4

Do you agree that Shakespeare is right not to lead straight from the Willow scene into the murder?

Ronald Draper

Ronald Draper is Regius Professor of Literature at the University of Aberdeen, and the author of numerous scholarly publications.

ESSAY

Unholy alliance: Othello and Iago

In his opening scene with Roderigo, Iago has to justify his contention that he holds Othello in his hate (I.1.6) despite the fact that he continues to follow him. 'I follow him to serve my turn upon him' (I.1.42) he says, and then goes on to contrast faithful servants, whose reward at the end of long service is to be fired, with those who pretend loyalty only to line their own pockets. It is the second kind that he himself belongs to, 'For, sir,' he says:

> It is as sure as you are Roderigo,
> Were I the Moor, I would not be Iago:
> In following him, I follow but myself.
> Heaven is my judge, not I for love and duty,
> But seeming so for my peculiar end:
> For when my outward action doth demonstrate
> The native act and figure of my heart
> In compliment extern, 'tis not long after,
> But I will wear my heart upon my sleeve
> For daws to peck at — I am not what I am.
>
> (I.1.57–66)

This seems blunt and plain-speaking, and yet it is professing duplicity with what sounds like contempt for direct, open behaviour. Its essence is that Iago himself is not what he appears to be, and that nobody worth his salt would dream of letting others see what he is really like. 'Love and duty' as such command no respect from Iago; he merely makes use of the appearance of them to serve his own ends. And to express this contrast he is fond of paradoxical, seemingly contradictory statements: 'In following him, I follow but myself', 'I am not what I am' — figures which in their very syntactical forms embody the opposition between appearance and reality on which his life seems to be based.

In the process of this self-exposition, Iago produces statements which seem obvious enough, but which manage nevertheless to be puzzling and peculiarly disturbing. 'Were I the Moor, I would not be Iago' is a particular example of this. Kenneth Muir makes short shrift of its meaning, glossing it simply as 'if I were the General, I would not wish to be a subordinate'[1] (though it is worth noting that this depends on reading 'would not be' in the sense of 'not willing, or wanting, to be', and 'Iago' as symbolic of man in an inferior position). M R Ridley, on the other hand, comments: 'This is not, I think, such plain sailing as the silence of most commentators suggests. To say "If I were the master, I would not be the man" sounds an oddly feeble remark from Iago. But it may be noticed that Shakespeare seems to have deliberately given Iago a trick of speech by which he makes remarks which appear at first hearing well-turned and significant, and on examination turn out to mean very little.'[2] Both commentators recognise a certain deviousness in what Iago says, though Ridley, I think, is the one who more truly reflects the uneasiness which we feel about this statement despite its seeming on the surface otiose and almost banal. Neither commentator, however, has anything to say about the relationship between Othello and Iago on which the words are focused and to which the whole discussion of leaders and followers, masters and men, is related.

---

[1] New Penguin edition of *Othello* (Harmondsworth, 1968), p. 182.
[2] The Arden edition of *Othello*, Methuen (London, 1958, paperback 1965), p. 7.

Iago's feeling towards Othello seems to be a contradictory mixture of envy and resentment. Part of his acknowledged motivation for conspiring against his commander derives from his sense of injured merit as a result of being passed over for the position of Lieutenant in favour of Cassio, part, as later suggested, from his suspicion that he has been cuckolded by Othello. The latter seems highly implausible; and even Iago's resentment at failure to secure promotion is for many commentators on the play so inadequate as an explanation of his behaviour that they fall back instead on Coleridge's celebrated 'motiveless malignity'. Yet what both motives imply, and likewise Iago's preoccupation with his status as a subordinate officer, is that he feels himself very closely linked to Othello. 'Were I the Moor' is an unspoken assumption behind much of what Iago says and does, and the complementary 'I would not be Iago' expresses his gnawing consciousness of being in some way belittled and made the victim of injustice by his existing position *vis à vis* Othello. Either way, his mind seems to be fixated on their relationship. It is already the focus of all his feelings, and in subsequent scenes of the play it will be the focus of all his actions.

Inferiority and superiority, with Othello as his standard of comparison, are a constant preoccupation of Iago's. What he thinks of his General is frankly enough revealed in his soliloquy at the end of Act I scene 3:

> The Moor is of a free and open nature,
> That thinks men honest that but seem to be so,
> And will as tenderly be led by th'nose
> As asses are.

(I.3.393–396)

In contrast with Iago's avowed use of appearances to deceive, which he presents to Roderigo in I.1 as something to be proud of, this frankness and openness of Othello's is seen as something to be despised. What would conventionally be regarded as virtuous is seen by the Italianate Iago, who in his Machiavellian fashion cultivates a 'politic' air of cynicism about human nature, as merely a form of weakness. He is confident that he knows the world much better than the man he is supposed to look up to as his leader; and he also sees that ignorance of the world on Othello's part as offering him a means to avenge himself for the way his own merits have been underestimated. By exploiting it Iago will be able to reverse their roles: he will become the leader and Othello will become the ass naïvely allowing himself to be led.

Of course, this attitude of Iago's is not confined to Othello. It is also the basis of his relationship with Roderigo ('Thus do I ever make my fool my purse:/ For I mine own gained knowledge should profane/ If I would time expend with such a snipe/ But for my sport and profit', I.3.377–380) and the cause of his resentment towards Cassio's promotion. He despises what he considers to be Cassio's merely theoretical knowledge of military matters — he is a fellow:

> That never set a squadron in the field,
> Nor the division of a battle knows
> More than a spinster — unless the bookish theoric,
> Wherein the togèd consuls can propose
> As masterly as he. Mere prattle without practice
> Is all his soldiership.

>   (I.1.22–27)

This has all the stinging contempt of an NCO in the field for the staff officer at HQ; but in Iago's case it also betrays again his sense of injured merit. He feels that his experience of actual warfare makes him superior to Cassio; whether or not justified in so thinking (and we find that the Venetian senate has a high opinion of Cassio's ability as a commander), he is persuaded that he is the better man and deserves recognition as such.

Such a belief in his own superiority may well, psychologically, be an indication of a deep-rooted sense of inferiority; but, in any case, it is an important clue to Iago's conduct. He feels the compulsion to denigrate others in order to elevate himself. With respect to Othello, his almost instinctive reaction is to undermine the foundations of his master's confidence while seeming to have his best interests at heart, which it is the easier for him to do because he is too cynical to be impressed by the grand rhetorical manner that enables Othello to make such an impact on others. Iago is compulsively reductive; he inhabits a world which is to him nothing but selfish and materialistic. As he crisply, and condescendingly (but with a highly characteristic quality of vicious energy), explains to Roderigo, moral considerations are irrelevant to him: ''Tis in ourselves that we are thus, or thus. Our bodies are our gardens, to the which our wills are gardeners.' (I.3.316–318). The exalted sentiment of 'love' on which Othello and Desdemona base their lives is a mere illusion to him, which time is bound to dispel; and the perverted energy of his language again reveals the supercilious contempt he feels for the emotional dupe he takes Othello to be: 'The food that to him now is as luscious as locusts shall be to him shortly as acerbe as the coloquintida' (I.3.343–345). Othello is reduced to 'an erring barbarian' and Desdemona to 'a super-subtle Venetian', and both, far from being 'too hard' for his 'wits', are, he boasts, putty in his hands. Intelligence, cynicism and superiority fuse together, making Iago his own forceful anti-hero.

The reductive cast of Iago's mind is clearly expressed in the satirically coarse language he uses to insinuate to Brabantio that his daughter has eloped with Othello: 'Even now, now, very now, an old black ram/ Is tupping your white ewe' and 'you'll have your daughter covered with a Barbary horse; you'll have your nephews neigh to you, you'll have coursers for cousins, and jennets for germans' (I.1.89–90, 111–114). But when it comes to the great scene of perverse intimacy between Iago and Othello (III.3), Iago begins his task of poisoning Othello's mind with deliberately underplayed language. A mere 'Ha! I like not that' is all he mutters when Cassio makes his exit at III.3.35, but, of course, it is calculated to arouse the sleeping suspicion of Othello. And again, after the dialogue between Othello and Desdemona in which Desdemona in complete innocence almost overdoes her pleading for Cassio's reinstatement, it is with a seemingly casual, unforced query, 'Did Michael Cassio,/ When you wooed my lady, know of your love?' (lines 93–94), that Iago resumes his puncturing of Othello's belief in his wife. Reluctance, cautious handling of suspicion, circumspection — not at all the blatant cynicism displayed in other contexts — are the impressions Iago seeks to cultivate, with exactly the result on which he calculates, namely that Othello credits him with the hesitant doubts of a completely loyal subordinate. Yet he massages Othello's anxiety with the utmost skill, even adopting a mask of frankness which entails admitting to the 'vice' of undue suspiciousness in order to seem, ironically, the more of a self-doubting subordinate, while tantalising his master with seemingly unspoken thoughts. Only when Othello has been brought to a state of puzzled dependency, apparently commanding ('By heaven, I'll know thy thoughts', linr 160), yet, in effect, begging for, greater outspokenness, does Iago release his own capacity for rhetorical colour:

> O, beware, my lord, of jealousy!
> It is the green-eyed monster, which doth mock
> The meat it feeds on.

(lines 163–165)

Othello's response to this is to match it with his customary grandeur and air of assurance:

> Think'st thou I'd make a life of jealousy,
> To follow still the changes of the moon
> With fresh suspicions? No, to be once in doubt
> Is once to be resolved. Exchange me for a goat,
> When I shall turn the business of my soul
> To such exsufflicate and blown surmises,
> Matching thy inference.

(lines 175–181)

He affirms his belief in the value of knowing the truth rather than lingering in uncertainty, and in his own power of self-control — again, the virtues of the leader. But the rhetorical question with which he asserts this (a question requiring the answer 'No', and here getting it from Othello himself) suggests nonetheless that a need is being felt for reassurance from the subordinate he is addressing; and his declaration:

> Nor from mine own weak merits will I draw
> The smallest fear or doubt of her revolt,
> For she had eyes and chose me

(lines 185–187)

though it sounds properly firm, opens up the very doubt it is meant to crush. Iago immediately recognises this, and via a touch of flattery for Othello's 'free and noble nature' (line 197, echoing, in the audience's ears, the 'free and open nature' sneered at previously) he pounces on the vulnerability it betrays with 'She did deceive her father, marrying you' (line 204).

That Iago is gaining the ascendancy is also revealed in his shifting from a posture of reluctant yielding to Othello's orders to a position in which he, in effect, issues them himself. 'Look to your wife,' he can now tell his master, 'observe her well with Cassio'. And the imperatives continue with 'Wear your eye thus: not jealous, nor secure' (lines 195–196). In raising the question of Desdemona's judgement in choosing Othello for her husband he senses that he has almost overstepped the mark, and he promptly beats something of a retreat (lines 209–211). For a while he returns to a more deferential mode of address: 'I hope you will consider what is spoke/ Comes from my love . . . I am to pray you . . .' (lines 214–216). However, seeing that his insinuations are starting to do their work, he is 'bold' (his own word at line 226) to revert to the dangerous issue of marital choice, this time inserting some of his own native reductiveness of language: 'One may smell in such a will most rank' (line 230). Retreat again follows, but he is soon issuing orders once more — even to the extent of telling Othello what to do about the reinstatement of his Lieutenant and the view he should take of Desdemona (lines 242–250). The upshot is Othello's 'Fear not my government' — a word that must mean primarily 'There's no need to doubt my self-control', but which also carries overtones of authority and power. It is these very things that Iago has now begun not only to subject to doubt, but even, in some measure, to transfer to himself. He has both the greater self-government and the greater authority; it is Iago who is usurping the seat of power.

In the earlier scenes of the play Othello is cool and commanding, unruffled and assured; his confidence issues in the superb understatement of 'Keep up your bright swords, for the dew will rust them' (I.2.59). At the same time the famous 'Othello music', counterpointing the 'rudeness' of speech (I.3.81) which belongs to his simplicity of character rather than his actual choice of vocabulary and phrasing, with its 'disastrous chances', 'moving accidents by flood and field' and 'hair-breadth scapes i'th'imminent deadly breach' (I.3.133–135), becomes a rhetorical projection of his warm, romantic nature. Iago, on the other hand, is scurrilous and foul-mouthed as befits his cynicism, while managing to seem frank and 'honest'. However, as the subordinate begins to gain ascendancy over the master, the warmth of Othello begins to take on the seething, chaotic heat of Iago's debased language of sexual innuendo, and his soaring magniloquence converts into histrionic melodrama ('Arise, black vengeance, from thy hollow cell!', III.3.444). And by the same token Iago acquires something of the high-flown rhetoric of Othello, particularly as their deepening relationship reaches its obscene climax in their joint swearing of vows. As Othello kneels to engage himself 'by yond marble heaven' to vengeance 'In the due reverence of a sacred vow' (lines 457–458), Iago kneels down beside him, likewise calling heaven to witness his oath:

> Witness you ever-burning lights above,
> You elements, that clip us round about,
> Witness that here Iago doth give up
> The execution of his wit, hands, heart,
> To wronged Othello's service. Let him command,
> And to obey shall be in me remorse,
> What bloody business ever.

> (lines 460–466)

In particular, the 'command'/'obey' antithesis underlines ironically the reversal of roles that has taken place in this parody of a religious ritual. Words and action combine to signal the creation of an unholy alliance in which the senior partner is nominally Othello, but in which control has in reality passed to Iago.

Thereafter, as has often been noted, Othello's great façade collapses. As a result of Iago's taunting use of the handkerchief, he slides from verse into prose and falls into an epileptic fit (IV.1.35–43); in the presence of the Venetian ambassadors, he insults Desdemona and strikes her, and makes his exit with an incoherent exclamation of 'Goats and monkeys!' (IV.1.465) (unconscious echo, perhaps, of Iago's 'It is impossible you should see this,/ Were they [Cassio and Desdemona] as prime as goats, as hot as monkeys', III.3.399–400); and he unwittingly acts out his own deterioration as he jeeringly treats Desdemona and Emilia as prostitute and bawd, and refers to his own corruption in terms of a poisoned fountain:

> But there where I have garnered up my heart,
> Where either I must live, or bear no life,

The fountain from the which my current runs,
Or else dries up — to be discarded thence
Or keep it as a cistern for foul toads
To knot and gender in!

(IV.2.56–61)

The Iago world of cynicism and sexual depravity has now become the world Othello's imagination inhabits. We see him as the poisoned victim rather than the dominant man of action, his mind turned inwards on his sense of horror and personal wrong. Iago himself, however, scurries still more actively and vigorously about the stage, contriving his plot to dispose of Roderigo and Cassio simultaneously, and twisting the screw on Othello still tighter — not, it must be admitted, totally in control as the executant of a perfectly conceived master-plan, but rather as a brilliant, yet slightly desperate, improviser, living on the brink at times of imminent disaster. But this, too, is of the nature of command, especially in the military field, where rapid adjustment to ever-changing conditions is indispensable. Iago contrives repeatedly to put himself in the position of the man who takes charge, and others seem naturally to look to him to do so. His 'honesty' here is not only his truthfulness, openness and trustworthiness, but also his resourcefulness and reliability — in the eyes, that is, of those around him. Indeed, it is at least in some degree his very consciousness of his thwarted talent to make others dance to his tune, his unfulfilled executive ability, the reality of which is demonstrated in this devilish activity, that motivates Iago and fuels his malice. His perverse triumph is to find an outlet for that talent in his treacherous 'service' of Othello, and in the process to take to himself the commanding role assigned to his master.

However, the curious relationship between Othello and Iago is not to be explained solely in terms of Iago's 'malcontent' syndrome. It is not only Othello's leadership which excites Iago's attention. The love between Othello and Desdemona is equally provocative; there is an instinctive hostility in Iago to the refinement of emotion on which romantic love depends, and he wishes not only to usurp the command of Othello, but also to 'set down the pegs that make' the 'music' of the latter's rapturous harmony with Desdemona. And there is perhaps an element of sexual rivalry present in his feelings too — though the existence of this is less easy to prove since Iago is less explicit on the subject. He speaks of the Moor as sexual rival for the favours of Emilia, but this is hardly convincing, given the emotional detachment Iago exhibits towards his wife. His antennae seem far more alert to Othello. It is, of course, an essential part of the deceptive act originally avowed to Roderigo in I.1 that he should seem attentive to Othello and alert to all that constitutes his welfare; and the culmination of this act is the scene of almost religious dedication already discussed and related to Iago's usurpation of command. But that scene, like so much in the play, is double-edged. It is not incompatible with the interpretation already advanced to suggest that it is also a kind of declaration of love, though the word 'love' itself has to be accepted as highly ambiguous in such a context. It may be argued that Iago is only pretending devotion, and parodying Othello's grandiloquence in the process; to concede this, however, is not to deny that the scene also generates an intensity of emotion which seems to mark the sealing of a profound bond of union between the two men. The act becomes a kind of reality in which both are convincingly caught up.

Again, 'love' in this context need not be construed as having specifically homosexual implications. A production of the play which chose to present the Othello–Iago relationship in such terms could, of course, be made to work, but the text does not afford any categorical evidence that this is how it should be played. What does emerge clearly enough, however, is that the intimacy between the two is greater than in any other relationship which the play presents, including that between Othello and Desdemona. The two men share intensely private and personal experiences — or, rather, Iago causes Othello to make confessions to him of a very private nature, and for his own part he makes private and personal admissions which, if they do not reveal his most intimate thoughts, do have the air of reluctantly 'honest' revelations. Both men are on stage, that is to say, in long stretches of dialogue which have the effect of seeming to pull them closer and closer together until the relationship between them becomes even more than that of commander to subordinate, or soldier-comrade to soldier-comrade. The magnificent climax of III.3:

> OTHELLO Now art thou my Lieutenant.
>
> IAGO I am your own for ever

has the high excitement of a mutual pact of blood brotherhood.
Iago, in particular, somehow contrives to make his declaration
to help Othello in what, after all, is no more than a matter of
supposed cuckoldry, sound more splendidly, and reverberate
with even greater emotional intensity, than a lover's avowal of
devotion and fidelity to his mistress. He lifts himself by the
sheer virtue of his rhetoric and play-acting to the level of
Othello's soul-mate.

Before the end of the play Othello is, of course, disabused;
but not until Iago's entwining himself with his master and
inverting of their relationship has done its work. Its ultimate
consummation is effected in that gross parody of consummation
(as commentators have noticed, there seems in the play's time-
scheme to be no opportunity for any other) which is embodied in
Othello's falsely exalted sacrifice of Desdemona. The relationship
between husband and wife is one of non-communication, or at
best frustrated communication; Othello listens to Iago as he
never listens to Desdemona, and it is this listening to the one
and failure to listen to the other which destroys him. When he
understands what he has done, he is possessed with almost
superhuman horror and self-loathing, but he achieves no greater
insight into Desdemona's nature. What his language focuses on
is his own damnation:

> Whip me, ye devils,
> From the possession of this heavenly sight!
> Blow me about in winds! Roast me in sulphur!
> Wash me in steep-down gulfs of liquid fire!
>
> (V.2.275–278)

And his last reference to Iago is a question in which he identifies
his tormentor:

> Will you, I pray, demand that demi-devil
> Why he hath thus ensnared my soul and body?
>
> (lines 298–299)

At this point the formerly so volubly confidential Iago jettisons
their intimacy, and with it any further communication what-
soever:

> Demand me nothing; what you know, you know:
> From this time forth I never will speak word.
>
> (lines 300–301)

But it is an essential part of the peculiar tragedy that is Othello's that he does not know what he knows. He has allowed Iago to become his mentor and soul-mate, but has never been able to understand in all its dire complexity exactly what has been done to him. He has submitted himself to a kind of psychological castration in which he has been robbed of his essential power and authority, and been seduced into a deep emotional intimacy which should have been reserved for another relationship.

AFTERTHOUGHTS

1

How would *you* interpret 'Were I the Moor, I would not be Iago' (page 107)?

2

What do you understand by 'Iago is compulsively reductive' (page 109)?

3

Which 'religious ritual' does Iago's speech quoted on page 113 seem to you to be parodying?

4

Do you agree that the intimacy between Othello and Iago is 'greater than in any other relationship which the play presents' (page 115)?

Neil Taylor

Neil Taylor is Dean of Arts and Humanities at Roehampton Institute. He is the author of numerous critical works.

ESSAY

'Look well to their linen'

Othello, like *Troilus and Cressida*, is much concerned with male notions of property. In Othello's imagination the Desdemona whom he kills is a pearl which he throws away (V.2.343); in Troilus's imagination the Cressida he yearns for is a pearl which he voyages to India to obtain (I.1.105).

Troilus also describes Helen of Troy as a pearl. She is one 'Whose price hath launched above a thousand ships,/ And turned crowned kings to merchants' (II.2.82–83). The imagery implies that women are merely merchandise and the action centres upon an act of trade: Helen's move from Greece to Troy is balanced by Cressida's move from the Trojan camp to the Greek camp. It is a kind of exchange, following in a sequence of exchanges. Her father changed sides and when she follows it takes the form of a literal handing over of a possession, the trading of a life for a life:

> Here is the lady
> Which for Antenor we deliver you.
> At the port, lord, I'll give her to thy hand,
> And by the way possess thee what she is.

(IV.4.109–112)

The succeeding scene emblematises the nature of any exchange-system:

AGAMEMNON   Is this the Lady Cressid?

DIOMEDES   Even she.

AGAMEMNON   Most *dearly* welcome to the Greeks, sweet lady.
   (*kisses her*)

NESTOR   Our general doth salute you with a kiss.

ULYSSES   Yet is the kindness but particular,
   'Twere better she were kissed in general.

(IV.5.17–21)

So it is that Cressida is passed on from Troilus to Diomedes to
Agamemnon to Nestor to Achilles to Patroclus, who kisses her
for Menelaus and for Paris. She moves from lip to lip like
language, and from hand to hand like money.

Thomas Rymer, writing *A Short View of Tragedy* in 1693, was
famously derisory of *Othello*:

> So much ado, so much stress, so much passion and repetition
> about an Handkerchief! Why was not this call'd the *Tragedy of
> the Handkerchief*? ... We have heard of *Fortunatis his Purse* ...
> but the Handkerchief is so remote a trifle, no Booby on this side
> *Mauretania* cou'd make any consequence from it.

For all his scorn, Rymer made a helpful suggestion when he
compared the handkerchief to a purse. The purse is not just a
piece of valuable private property for the characters in the play,
it is used by Shakespeare as a device for defining the ethos of
the city in which the action has its origins. 'Put money in thy
purse,' is Iago's famous advice to Roderigo (I.3.336), and it is a
philosophy well suited to Venice, a trading city located at the
cross-roads of the Mediterranean.

   The mercantile ethos of Shakespeare's Venice and the
financial basis of Elizabethan marriage combine in Brabantio's
accusation that Othello is a 'foul thief' for having married his
daughter (I.2.62). Othello shares in this conception, yet, in a
paradoxical way, can ignore it. He would not mind, he explains,
if the whole of his army tasted Desdemona's sweet body! He
would not mind, just so long as he did not *know* (III.3.342–343).
But he comes to believe that he does know, and what makes the
torment of knowing greater is the idea that property can always
be traded. Brabantio points it out: 'She has deceived her father,

and may thee' (I.3.290). Othello is confronted with the tormenting image of Desdemona continuously changing hands like Cressida, and like money.

The idea that she is his property has come to be the very basis of Othello's sense of Venetian identity. So, when he is persuaded by Iago that his 'occupation' (a pun, meaning both his job and his sexual partner) has gone (III.3.354), chaos is come again. Without his occupation, he might as well have lost his place in the universe itself. He is no longer Othello, and begins to refer to himself in the third person:

> That's he that *was* Othello . . .
>
> (V.2.281, my italics)

Iago typifies Venetian values insofar as his mind runs on the idea of exchange in one office or another, and his language deals frequently in monetary images. He claims that Cassio has stolen his job and Othello has stolen his wife. He controls Roderigo's purse as if the strings were his own (I.1.2–3) and he knows his price (I.1.11). He tortures Othello by referring to his honour as his most valued piece of property, 'the immediate jewel' of his soul:

> Who steals my purse, steals trash; 'tis something, nothing;
> 'Twas mine, 'tis his, and has been slave to thousands:
> But he that filches from me my good name
> Robs me of that which not enriches him
> And makes me poor indeed.
>
> (III.3.156–160)

When Iago calls money 'trash' we remember that he uses the same term of Roderigo (II.1.294) and that he had anyway called Roderigo his purse at I.3.377. A purse not only is and stands for property, it is a stage-property — like the famous handkerchief.

The handkerchief, like the purse, is a valued stage-property whose narrative not only helps determine the outcome of the plot but provides a further metaphor for the value-system of Venice.

It is no ordinary handkerchief. Its pattern of strawberries is beautiful and Cassio would have Bianca copy it (III.4.186–187). It is something to look at and it is pictorial, representational. It is therefore to be read. But how is one to read it and its enigmatic pattern? Iago takes advantage of its nature, reading into it for Othello a significance it need not have.

And Iago works in this way always. In Act III scene 3, the scene in which he later introduces mention of the handkerchief, he practises the tricks of his trade by tempting Othello to consider carefully what would otherwise have been unconsidered trifles of language:

> IAGO I did not think he had been *acquainted* with her.
> OTHELLO O yes, and *went between us* very oft.
> IAGO *Indeed?*
> OTHELLO Indeed? [*In deed?*] Ay, indeed! [*In deed!*] Discern'st thou aught in that? Is he not honest?
> IAGO *Honest,* my lord?
>
> (lines 98–102, my italics)

Iago offers *acquainted*, calls attention to *went between us* and echoes *honest* — making something sexual out of *acquainted*, seeing the trading of *went between us* as an act of sexual intervention and questioning the scope of Othello's understanding of what *honest* can mean. Most brilliant of all is his making two words out of one in *indeed*.

Iago's greatest achievement is to sell Othello this very skill in punning and irony. And Othello's richest use of it is when he questions Desdemona about the handkerchief:

> OTHELLO Give me your hand. This hand is moist, my lady.
> DESDEMONA It hath felt no age, nor known no sorrow.
> OTHELLO This argues fruitfulness and liberal heart.
>   Hot, hot and moist. This hand of yours requires
>   A sequester from liberty, fasting and prayer,
>   Much castigation, exercise devout;
>   For there's a young and sweating devil here
>   That commonly rebels. 'Tis a good hand,
>   A frank one.
>
> (III.4.36–44)

Othello's pain derives from reading into *liberty* and *liberality* 'licence' and 'licentiousness'. Where *free* can mean 'pure and virtuous' and 'in a state of grace', Othello has been persuaded it means 'sexually dishonest'. Where *frank* can mean 'honest',

Othello wishes it also to mean 'boldly loose with its favours'. And, of course, the hand he is holding *is* ambiguous — what he takes to be the sweat of sexual arousal is equally to be read as the sweat of fear. The fear of assault is for him the fear of guilt. Because he fears she is too freely handled, handed on from hand to hand, he is finally driven to strike her with his hand.

In the meanwhile he concentrates on the handkerchief. She first produced it at III.3.284, to bind his forehead which suffers from the forked plague. That she drops it would have interested Freud. Could it be that she intends to lose it? Is there something in her relationship to Othello that she wishes to lose? Is she bound to him in a way that is intolerable? The answers are all probably yes. But Shakespeare leaves this event as ambiguous as the handkerchief itself:

> OTHELLO   Your napkin is too little;
> Let it alone.

> III.3.284–285

Is 'it' his forehead or the handkerchief? If the latter, does he push it to the floor? Is she being commanded to lose it? Is it a trifle to him? Surely not. The handkerchief is precious to him, or so he claims. Not just beautiful but unique, and therefore priceless. Is she jealous of his relationship with it? If so, no wonder if she does indeed lose it with unconscious deliberation.

Because it is so precious the handkerchief becomes the symbol of all that's precious in the play — Desdemona, the pearl; Desdemona's honour; Desdemona's life; Othello's honour; Othello's sense of ownership; Othello's sense of identity. All that is lost:

> OTHELLO   Make it a darling like your precious eye.
> To lose or give't away were such perdition
> As nothing else could match.
> DESDEMONA   Is't possible?
> OTHELLO   'Tis true: there's magic in the web of it.
> A sibyl, that had numbered in the world
> The sun to course two hundred compasses,
> In her prophetic fury sewed the work
>
>   . . .
>
> DESDEMONA   Indeed? Is't true?

> (III.4.66–75)

Is it true? The handkerchief has suddenly come to symbolise something new — the hold Othello has over Desdemona. And that hold — ironically he is standing there with his hand out to her, empty-handed ('Lend me thy handkerchief', III.4.52) — is not physical. She is psychologically held, as Brabantio and the Duke of Venice were in Act I scene 3, and as she always has been held by Othello, by his words, by his stories, by his ideas, by his imagination.

As with Iago's ideas about adultery, we cannot know the truth of Othello's statements. Did a sibyl make it? Is it really so rare, so precious? In the other play, Troilus wisely asked 'What's aught but as 'tis valued?' (II.2.51). Because he is her husband, Desdemona is forced to give the handkerchief Othello's valuation. Now she will even lie to protect its value. Price and value must now occupy her thoughts and she will spend her last hours debating with Emilia whether the world is 'a great price for a small vice' (IV.3.67–68) and what it is that husbands do 'When they change us for others' (IV.3.96).

It is Emilia's opinion that she might abuse her husband for the world, but not 'for measures of lawn' (IV.3.71). The brilliance of the handkerchief as a device in the play is that, in its passivity, it exemplifies the whole nature of exchange. It operates as money, as portable property. Everyone has, or surely will, handle and temporarily own that handkerchief. It passes on from hand to hand like Cressida. A sibyl handed it to an Egyptian, who handed it on to Othello's father. From him it moved to Othello's mother, to Othello and then to Desdemona. She lost it but it was found by Emilia, who handed it to Iago, who passed it on to Cassio, who gave it to Bianca to copy. Had she done so she would have been characteristically debasing the coinage. *That*, says Iago to Othello, is how your wife behaves (IV.1.172–176).

In Shakespeare's day it would still, presumably, have been meaningful to debate the intrinsic value as opposed to the ascribed value of the coinage, but the intrinsic value ultimately derives from the market too. Troilus and Othello are both asked to comprehend how such a system works and, at the same time, how they operate within, as well as upon, the system. Troilus is incapable of coming to terms with Cressida's behaviour. For him she is false. We, on the other hand, might regard her as just as true as Troilus. Othello loses his belief in Desdemona's chastity. We never do. It is as if she were our property and we cannot bear to let her go. Yet we can never prove her chaste. The truth in her story is as enigmatic as the figure in the carpet in Henry James's story of that name. As enigmatic, in fact, as the strawberry pattern in the handkerchief.

Since we can never be proved wrong, we may be permitted to speculate about Othello's readings of the pattern. Perhaps, when he watches the handkerchief float to the ground, he thinks of the 'lightness' and infidelity of his wife. Perhaps, though, he sees himself in it, saying to Desdemona 'Just as my father blackmailed my mother with this white cloth, I am saying don't lose it or you lose me.' Perhaps, again, he sees in it himself *and* Desdemona, seeing white sheets spotted with blood and thinking 'Tonight we were going to consummate our marriage'.

T G A Nelson and Charles Haines have argued ('Othello's Unconsummated Marriage', *Essays in Criticism* XXXIII, January 1983, no. 1) that Othello and Desdemona never have time to consummate their marriage. The red-spotted handkerchief 'objectifies Othello's fear that the privilege of taking Desdemona's maidenhead has likewise fallen to another man (specifically to Cassio, into whose possession the handkerchief comes)' (p. 2). The handkerchief thus becomes an agent of torment to Othello whose 'rational faculties are clouded . . . by unbearable frustration' (p. 13). As Othello puts it, in characteristic financial imagery:

> The purchase made, the fruits are to ensue:
> The profit's yet to come 'tween me and you.

(II.3.9–10)

Othello knows that at the 'compt' (V.2.271) he and Desdemona will be divorced eternally. In his final statement to those who will judge him on earth, he casts himself in three roles: no longer the Christian any more but the Judean who 'threw a pearl away/ Richer than all his tribe' (V.2.343–344); no longer the Venetian any more but 'a turbaned Turk . . . [who] traduced the state' (lines 349–350); no longer the husband any more who could not consummate his marriage but the lover who finds the truest consummation in death, dying upon a kiss (line 355). He stabs himself to make a tragic loading of the marriage bed:

LODOVICO   O bloody period!

(line 353)

The sheets are stained at last. A copy of the handkerchief has been made after all, enlarged for all to see. Perhaps one day a director of *Othello* will end the play, not just with Lodovico exemplifying Venetian priorities by telling Gratiano to 'seize upon the fortunes of the Moor' (line 362), but with a public display of Desdemona's wedding sheets, spotted at last with lust's blood, emblematising the handkerchief as much as ever the handkerchief emblematised it.

AFTERTHOUGHTS

1

What is the function of the references in this essay to *Troilus and Cressida*? How helpful do you find them?

2

What do you understand by Taylor's reference to Freud (page 123)?

3

'It operates as money, as portable property' (page 124). Do you agree with Taylor's analysis of the handkerchief in *Othello* as exemplifying 'the nature of exchange'?

4

Explain the significance that has been suggested for the strawberry motif on the handkerchief (pages 125–126). Are you convinced?

INTRODUCTION

First, a word of warning. Good essays are the product of a creative engagement with literature. So never try to restrict your studies to what you think will be 'useful in the exam'. Ironically, you will restrict your grade potential if you do.

This doesn't mean, of course, that you should ignore the basic skills of essay writing. When you read critics, make a conscious effort to notice *how* they communicate their ideas. The guidelines that follow offer advice of a more explicit kind. But they are no substitute for practical experience. It is never easy to express ideas with clarity and precision. But the more often you tackle the problems involved and experiment to find your own voice, the more fluent you will become. So practise writing essays as often as possible.

HOW TO PLAN
AN ESSAY

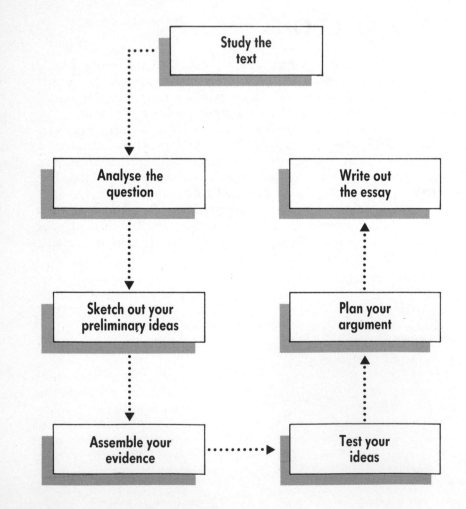

```
                    ┌──────────────┐
            ┌·······│  Study the   │
            :       │     text     │
            :       └──────────────┘
            ▼
    ┌──────────────┐              ┌──────────────┐
    │ Analyse the  │              │  Write out   │
    │   question   │              │  the essay   │
    └──────────────┘              └──────────────┘
            :                             ▲
            ▼                             :
    ┌──────────────┐              ┌──────────────┐
    │ Sketch out your │           │  Plan your   │
    │ preliminary ideas │         │   argument   │
    └──────────────┘              └──────────────┘
            :                             ▲
            ▼                             :
    ┌──────────────┐              ┌──────────────┐
    │ Assemble your│·············▶│  Test your   │
    │   evidence   │              │    ideas     │
    └──────────────┘              └──────────────┘
```

Study the text

The first step in writing a good essay is to get to know the set text well. Never write about a text until you are fully familiar with it. Even a discussion of the opening chapter of a novel, for example, should be informed by an understanding of the book as a whole. Literary texts, however, are by their very nature complex and on a first reading you are bound to miss many significant features. Re-read the book with care, if possible more than once. Look up any unfamiliar words in a good dictionary and if the text you are studying was written more than a few decades ago, consult the *Oxford English Dictionary* to find out whether the meanings of any terms have shifted in the intervening period.

Good books are difficult to put down when you first read them. But a more leisurely second or third reading gives you the opportunity to make notes on those features you find significant. An index of characters and events is often useful, particularly when studying novels with a complex plot or time scheme. The main aim, however, should be to record your *responses* to the text. By all means note, for example, striking images. But be sure to add *why* you think them striking. Similarly, record any thoughts you may have on interesting comparisons with other texts, puzzling points of characterisation, even what you take to be aesthetic blemishes. The important thing is to annotate fully and adventurously. The most seemingly idiosyncratic comment may later lead to a crucial area of discussion which you would otherwise have overlooked. It helps to have a working copy of the text in which to mark up key passages and jot down marginal comments (although obviously these practices are taboo when working with library, borrowed or valuable copies!). But keep a fuller set of notes as well and organise these under appropriate headings.

Literature does not exist in an aesthetic vacuum, however, and you should try to find out as much as possible about the context of its production and reception. It is particularly important to read other works by the same author and writings by contemporaries. At this early stage, you may want to restrict your secondary reading to those standard reference works, such as biographies, which are widely available in public libraries. In the long run, however, it pays to read as wide a range of critical studies as possible.

Some students, and tutors, worry that such studies may stifle the development of any truly personal response. But this won't happen if you are alert to the danger and read critically. After all, you wouldn't passively accept what a stranger told you in conversation. The fact that a critic's views are in print does not necessarily make them any more authoritative (as a glance at the review pages of the *TLS* and *London Review of Books* will reveal). So question the views you find: 'Does this critic's interpretation agree with mine and where do we part company?' 'Can it be right to try and restrict this text's meanings to those found by its author or first audience?' 'Doesn't this passage treat a theatrical text as though it were a novel?' Often it is views which you reject which prove most valuable since they challenge you to articulate your own position with greater clarity. Be sure to keep careful notes on what the critic wrote, and your *reactions* to what the critic wrote.

Analyse the question

You cannot begin to answer a question until you understand what task it is you have been asked to perform. Recast the question in your own words and reconstruct the line of reasoning which lies behind it. Where there is a choice of topics, try to choose the one for which you are best prepared. It would, for example, be unwise to tackle 'How far do you agree that in *Paradise Lost* Milton transformed the epic models he inherited from ancient Greece and Rome?' without a working knowledge of Homer and Virgil (or *Paradise Lost* for that matter!). If you do not already know the works of these authors, the question should spur you on to read more widely — or discourage you from attempting it at all. The scope of an essay, however, is not always so obvious and you must remain alert to the implied demands of each question. How could you possibly 'Consider the view that *Wuthering Heights* transcends the conventions of the Gothic novel' without reference to at least some of those works which, the question suggests, have *not* transcended Gothic conventions?

When you have decided on a topic, analyse the terms of the question itself. Sometimes these self-evidently require careful definition: *tragedy* and *irony*, for example, are notoriously difficult concepts to pin down and you will probably need to consult a good dictionary of literary terms. Don't ignore, however, those seemingly innocuous phrases which often smuggle in significant assumptions. 'Does Macbeth lack the nobility of the true tragic hero?' obviously invites you to discuss nobility and the nature of the tragic hero. But what of 'lack' and 'true' — do they suggest that the play would be improved had Shakespeare depicted Macbeth in a different manner? or that tragedy is superior to other forms of drama? Remember that you are not expected meekly to agree with the assumptions implicit in the question. Some questions are deliberately provocative in order to stimulate an engaged response. Don't be afraid to take up the challenge.

Sketch out your preliminary ideas

'Which comes first, the evidence or the answer?' is one of those chicken and egg questions. How can you form a view without inspecting the evidence? But how can you know which evidence is relevant without some idea of what it is you are looking for? In practice the mind reviews evidence and formulates preliminary theories or hypotheses at one and the same time, although for the sake of clarity we have separated out the processes. Remember that these early ideas are only there to get you started. You *expect* to modify them in the light of the evidence you uncover. Your initial hypothesis may be an instinctive 'gut-reaction'. Or you may find that you prefer to 'sleep on the problem', allowing ideas to gell over a period of time. Don't worry in either case. The mind is quite capable of processing a vast amount of accumulated evidence, the product of previous reading and thought, and reaching sophisticated intuitive judgements. Eventually, however, you are going to have to think carefully through any ideas you arrive at by such intuitive processes. Are they logical? Do they take account of all the relevant factors? Do they fully answer the question set? Are there any obvious reasons to qualify or abandon them?

Assemble your evidence

Now is the time to return to the text and re-read it with the question and your working hypothesis firmly in mind. Many of the notes you have already made are likely to be useful, but assess the precise relevance of this material and make notes on any new evidence you discover. The important thing is to cast your net widely and take into account points which tend to undermine your case as well as those that support it. As always, ensure that your notes are full, accurate, and reflect your own critical judgements.

You may well need to go outside the text if you are to do full justice to the question. If you think that the 'Oedipus complex' may be relevant to an answer on *Hamlet* then read Freud and a balanced selection of those critics who have discussed the appropriateness of applying psychoanalytical theories to the interpretation of literature. Their views can most easily be tracked down by consulting the annotated bibliographies held by most major libraries (and don't be afraid to ask a librarian for help in finding and using these). Remember that you go to works of criticism not only to obtain information but to stimulate you into clarifying your own position. And that since life is short and many critical studies are long, judicious use of a book's index and/or contents list is not to be scorned. You can save yourself a great deal of future labour if you carefully record full bibliographic details at this stage.

Once you have collected the evidence, organise it coherently. Sort the detailed points into related groups and identify the quotations which support these. You must also assess the relative importance of each point, for in an essay of limited length it is essential to establish a firm set of priorities, exploring some ideas in depth while discarding or subordinating others.

Test your ideas

As we stressed earlier, a hypothesis is only a proposal, and one that you fully expect to modify. Review it with the evidence before you. Do you really still believe in it? It would be surprising if you did not want to modify it in some way. If you cannot see any problems, others may. Try discussing your ideas with friends and relatives. Raise them in class discussions. Your tutor is certain to welcome your initiative. The critical process is essentially collaborative and there is absolutely no reason why you should not listen to and benefit from the views of others. Similarly, you should feel free to test your ideas against the theories put forward in academic journals and books. But do not just borrow what you find. Critically analyse the views on offer and, where appropriate, integrate them into your own pattern of thought. You must, of course, give full acknowledgement to the sources of such views.

Do not despair if you find you have to abandon or modify significantly your initial position. The fact that you are prepared to do so is a mark of intellectual integrity. Dogmatism is never an academic virtue and many of the best essays explore the *process* of scholarly enquiry rather than simply record its results.

Plan your argument

Once you have more or less decided on your attitude to the question (for an answer is never really 'finalised') you have to present your case in the most persuasive manner. In order to do this you must avoid meandering from point to point and instead produce an organised argument — a structured flow of ideas and supporting evidence, leading logically to a conclusion which fully answers the question. Never begin to write until you have produced an outline of your argument.

You may find it easiest to begin by sketching out its main stage as a flow chart or some other form of visual presentation. But eventually you should produce a list of paragraph topics. The paragraph is the conventional written demarcation for a unit of thought and you can outline an argument quite simply by briefly summarising the substance of each paragraph and then checking that these points (you may remember your English teacher referring to them as topic sentences) really do follow a coherent order. Later you will be able to elaborate on each topic, illustrating and qualifying it as you go along. But you will find this far easier to do if you possess from the outset a clear map of where you are heading.

All questions require some form of an argument. Even so-called 'descriptive' questions *imply* the need for an argument. An adequate answer to the request to 'Outline the role of Iago in *Othello*' would do far more than simply list his appearances on stage. It would at the very least attempt to provide some *explanation* for his actions — is he, for example, a representative stage 'Machiavel'? an example of pure evil, 'motiveless malignity'? or a realistic study of a tormented personality reacting to identifiable social and psychological pressures?

Your conclusion ought to address the terms of the question. It may seem obvious, but 'how far do you agree', 'evaluate', 'consider', 'discuss', etc, are *not* interchangeable formulas and your conclusion must take account of the precise wording of the question. If asked 'How far do you agree?', the concluding paragraph of your essay really should state whether you are in complete agreement, total disagreement, or, more likely, partial agreement. Each preceding paragraph should have a clear justification for its existence and help to clarify the reasoning which underlies your conclusion. If you find that a paragraph serves no good purpose (perhaps merely summarising the plot), do not hesitate to discard it.

The arrangement of the paragraphs, the overall strategy of the argument, can vary. One possible pattern is dialectical: present the arguments in favour of one point of view (**thesis**); then turn to counter-arguments or to a rival interpretation (**antithesis**); finally evaluate the competing claims and arrive at your own conclusion (**synthesis**). You may, on the other hand, feel so convinced of the merits of one particular case that you wish to devote your entire essay to arguing that viewpoint persuasively (although it is always desirable to indicate, however briefly, that you are aware of alternative, if flawed, positions). As the essays contained in this volume demonstrate, there are many other possible strategies. Try to adopt the one which will most comfortably accommodate the demands of the question and allow you to express your thoughts with the greatest possible clarity.

Be careful, however, not to apply abstract formulas in a mechanical manner. It is true that you should be careful to define your terms. It is *not* true that every essay should begin with 'The dictionary defines *x* as . . .'. In fact, definitions are often best left until an appropriate moment for their introduction arrives. Similarly every essay should have a beginning, middle and end. But it does not follow that in your opening paragraph you should announce an intention to write an essay, or that in your concluding paragraph you need to signal an imminent desire to put down your pen. The old adages are often useful reminders of what constitutes good practice, but they must be interpreted intelligently.

Write out the essay

Once you have developed a coherent argument you should aim to communicate it in the most effective manner possible. Make certain you clearly identify yourself, and the question you are answering. Ideally, type your answer, or at least ensure your handwriting is legible and that you leave sufficient space for your tutor's comments. Careless presentation merely distracts from the force of your argument. Errors of grammar, syntax and spelling are far more serious. At best they are an irritating blemish, particularly in the work of a student who should be sensitive to the nuances of language. At worst, they seriously confuse the sense of your argument. If you are aware that you have stylistic problems of this kind, ask your tutor for advice at the earliest opportunity. Everyone, however, is liable to commit the occasional howler. The only remedy is to give yourself plenty of time in which to proof-read your manuscript (often reading it aloud is helpful) before submitting it.

Language, however, is not only an instrument of communication; it is also an instrument of thought. If you want to think clearly and precisely you should strive for a clear, precise prose style. Keep your sentences short and direct. Use modern, straightforward English wherever possible. Avoid repetition, clichés and wordiness. Beware of generalisations, simplifications, and overstatements. Orwell analysed the relationship between stylistic vice and muddled thought in his essay 'Politics and the English Language' (1946) — it remains essential reading (and is still readily available in volume 4 of the Penguin *Collected Essays, Journalism and Letters*). Generalisations, for example, are always dangerous. They are rarely true and tend to suppress the individuality of the texts in question. A remark such as 'Keats always employs sensuous language in his poetry' is not only fatuous (what, after all, does it mean? is *every* word he wrote equally 'sensuous'?) but tends to obscure interesting distinctions which could otherwise be made between, say, the descriptions in the 'Ode on a Grecian Urn' and those in 'To Autumn'.

The intelligent use of quotations can help you make your points with greater clarity. Don't sprinkle them throughout your essay without good reason. There is no need, for example, to use them to support uncontentious statements of fact. 'Macbeth murdered Duncan' does not require textual evidence (unless you wish to dispute Thurber's brilliant parody, 'The Great Macbeth Murder Mystery', which reveals Lady Macbeth's father as the culprit!). Quotations should be included, however, when they are necessary to support your case. The proposition that Macbeth's imaginative powers wither after he has killed his king would certainly require extensive quotation: you would almost certainly want to analyse key passages from both before and after the murder (perhaps his first and last soliloquies?). The key word here is 'analyse'. Quotations cannot make your points on their own. It is up to you to demonstrate their relevance and clearly explain to your readers *why* you want them to focus on the passage you have selected.

Most of the academic conventions which govern the presentation of essays are set out briefly in the style sheet below. The question of gender, however, requires fuller discussion. More than half the population of the world is female. Yet many writers still refer to an undifferentiated *man*kind. Or write of the author and *his* public. We do not think that this convention has much to recommend it. At the very least, it runs the risk of introducing unintended sexist attitudes. And at times leads to such patent absurdities as 'Cleopatra's final speech asserts *man*'s true nobility'. With a little thought, you can normally find ways of expressing yourself which do not suggest that the typical author, critic or reader is male. Often you can simply use plural forms, which is probably a more elegant solution than relying on such awkward formulations as 's/he' or 'he and she'. You should also try to avoid distinguishing between male and female authors on the basis of forenames. Why *Jane* Austen and not *George* Byron? Refer to all authors by their last names unless there is some good reason not to. Where there may otherwise be confusion, say between T S and George Eliot, give the name in full when if first occurs and thereafter use the last name only.

Finally, keep your audience firmly in mind. Tutors and examiners are interested in understanding your conclusions and the processes by which you arrived at them. They are not interested in reading a potted version of a book they already know. **So don't pad out your work with plot summary.**

Hints for examinations

In an examination you should go through exactly the same processes as you would for the preparation of a term essay. The only difference lies in the fact that some of the stages will have had to take place before you enter the examination room. This should not bother you unduly. Examiners are bound to avoid the merely eccentric when they come to formulate papers and if you have read widely and thought deeply about the central issues raised by your set texts you can be confident you will have sufficient material to answer the majority of questions sensibly.

The fact that examinations impose strict time limits makes it *more* rather than less, important that you plan carefully. There really is no point in floundering into an answer without any idea of where you are going, particularly when there will not be time to recover from the initial error.

Before you begin to answer any question at all, study the entire paper with care. Check that you understand the rubric and know how many questions you have to answer and whether any are compulsory. It may be comforting to spot a title you feel confident of answering well, but don't rush to tackle it: read *all* the questions before deciding which *combination* will allow you to display your abilities to the fullest advantage. Once you have made your choice, analyse each question, sketch out your ideas, assemble the evidence, review your initial hypothesis, plan your argument, *before* trying to write out an answer. And make notes at each stage: not only will these help you arrive at a sensible conclusion, but examiners are impressed by evidence of careful thought.

Plan your time as well as your answers. If you have practised writing timed essays as part of your revision, you should not find this too difficult. There can be a temptation to allocate extra time to the questions you know you can answer well; but this is always a short-sighted policy. You will find yourself left to face a question which would in any event have given you difficulty without even the time to give it serious thought. It is, moreover, easier to gain marks at the lower end of the scale than at the upper, and you will never compensate for one poor answer by further polishing two satisfactory answers. Try to leave some time at the end of the examination to re-read your answers and correct any obvious errors. If the worst comes to the worst and you run short of time, don't just keep writing until you are forced to break off in mid-paragraph. It is far better to provide for the examiner a set of notes which indicate the overall direction of your argument.

Good luck — but if you prepare for the examination conscientiously and tackle the paper in a methodical manner, you won't need it!

deceiving Benedick and Beatrice into 'a mountain of affection th'one with th'other' (II.1.339–340). The basis of both plots is getting the victims to overhear other people speaking, as they think, honestly.

In fact, therefore, we are being presented with two types of deceit: that which is benevolent, like Don Pedro's or the Friar's seeking ultimately a harmony that can be expressed [marriage], and that which is totally destructive, like Don [John]. The success of each type of deceit depends on a manipul[ation of] language and an alteration of behaviour and appearances [and] on the readiness of the victims to judge from what is pres[ented to] their eyes and ears. Telling the two types apart may [be diffi]cult.

[I]t is not as if any character is unaware of the difficult [relat]ionship of appearance to reality: but nearly every one is led [to] choose, of two alternatives, the wrong one. The best instance of this comes at the crisis of the play:

HERO   . . . seemed I ever otherwise to you?
CLAUDIO Out of thee! Seeming! I will write against it.
         You seem to me as Dian in her orb,
         As chaste as is the bud ere it be blown;
         But you are more intemperate in your blood
         Than Venus, or those pampered animals
         That rage in savage sensuality.

                                             (IV.1.53–59)

Hero's innocent use of the word 'seemed' — not 'was' — gets Claudio on the raw, for it raises the issue of behaviour versus real nature that is the cause of his torment. It triggers [a] remarkable anticipation of Othello's tortured animal im[agery] that highlights the emotional perception of the disju[nction] between appearance and what Claudio at this point beli[eves to] be reality. He could not be more wrong; and he is wrong [because] he trusted the suspect word of Don John and what he wa[s led] to see at Hero's window rather than the woman he chose to [have] as his wife. Love must, as both Desdemona (*Othello*) and Cordelia (*King Lear*) know, depend on trust: it (or its lack) can never be *proved*. Claudio is given 'ocular proof' (*Othello* III.3.360) of Hero's apparent unchastity, just as Othello is of Desdemona's by Iago, a stage-managing and manipulating

---

Annotations:

short prose quotation incorporated in the text of the essay, within quotation marks.

Three dots (ellipsis) indicate where words or phrases have been cut from a quotation or where (as here) a quotation begins mid-sentence.

long verse quotation indented and introduced by a colon. No quotation marks are needed.

Line reference given directly after the quotation, in brackets.

book/play titles are given in italics. In a handwritten or typed manuscript this would appear as underlining: King Lear; Othello.

Short verse quotation incorporated in the text of the essay within quotation marks. If the quotation ran on into a second line of poetry, this would be indicated by a slash (/).

We have divided the following information into two sections. Part A describes those rules which it is essential to master no matter what kind of essay you are writing (including examination answers). Part B sets out some of the more detailed conventions which govern the documentation of essays.

PART A: LAYOUT

Titles of texts

Titles of published books, plays (of any length), long poems, pamphlets and periodicals (including newspapers and magazines), works of classical literature, and films should be underlined: e.g. <u>David Copperfield</u> (novel), <u>Twelfth Night</u> (play), <u>Paradise Lost</u> (long poem), <u>Critical Quarterly</u> (periodical), Horace's <u>Ars Poetica</u> (Classical work), <u>Apocalypse Now</u> (film).

Notice how important it is to distinguish between titles and other names. <u>Hamlet</u> is the play; Hamlet the prince. <u>Wuthering Heights</u> is the novel; Wuthering Heights the house. Underlining is the equivalent in handwritten or typed manuscripts of printed italics. So what normally appears in this volume as *Othello* would be written as <u>Othello</u> in your essay.

Titles of articles, essays, short stories, short poems, songs, chapters of books, speeches, and newspaper articles are enclosed in quotation marks; e.g. 'The Flea' (short poem), 'The Prussian Officer' (short story), 'Middleton's Chess Strategies' (article), 'Thatcher Defects!' (newspaper headline).

Exceptions: Underlining titles or placing them within quotation marks does not apply to sacred writings (e.g. Bible, Koran, Old Testament, Gospels) or parts of a book (e.g. Preface, Introduction, Appendix).

It is generally incorrect to place quotation marks around a title of a published book which you have underlined. The exception is 'titles within titles': e.g. '<u>Vanity Fair</u>': A Critical Study (title of a book about *Vanity Fair*).

Quotations

Short verse quotations of a single line or part of a line should be incorporated within quotation marks as part of the running text of your essay. Quotations of two or three lines of verse are treated in the same way, with line endings indicated by a slash(/). For example:

1 In Julius Caesar, Antony says of Brutus, 'This was the noblest Roman of them all'.
2 The opening of Antony's famous funeral oration, 'Friends, Romans, Countrymen, lend me your ears;/ I come to bury Caesar not to praise him', is a carefully controlled piece of rhetoric.

Longer verse quotations of more than three lines should be indented from the main body of the text and introduced in most cases with a colon. Do not enclose indented quotations within quotation marks. For example:

It is worth pausing to consider the reasons Brutus gives to justify his decision to assassinate Caesar:

> It must be by his death; and for my part,
> I know no personal cause to spurn at him,
> But for the general. He would be crowned.
> How might that change his nature, there's the question.

At first glance his rationale may appear logical . . .

Prose quotations of less than three lines should be incorporated in the text of the essay, within quotation marks. Longer prose quotations should be indented and the quotation marks omitted. For example:

1 Before his downfall, Caesar rules with an iron hand. His political opponents, the Tribunes Marullus and Flavius, are 'put to silence' for the trivial offence of 'pulling scarfs off Caesar's image'.
2 It is interesting to note the rhetorical structure of Brutus's Forum speech:

> Romans, countrymen, and lovers, hear me for my cause, and be silent that you may hear. Believe me for my honour, and have respect to mine honour that you may believe. Censure me in your wisdom, and awake your senses, that you may the better judge.

Tenses: When you are relating the events that occur within a work of fiction or describing the author's technique, it is the convention to use the present tense. Even though Orwell published *Animal Farm* in 1945, the book *describes* the animals' seizure of Manor Farm. Similarly, Macbeth always *murders* Duncan, despite the passage of time.

PART B: DOCUMENTATION

When quoting from verse of more than twenty lines, provide line references: e.g. In 'Upon Appleton House' Marvell's mower moves 'With whistling scythe and elbow strong' (1.393).

Quotations from plays should be identified by act, scene and line references: e.g. Prospero, in Shakespeare's The Tempest, refers to Caliban as 'A devil, a born devil' (IV.1.188). (i.e. Act 4. Scene 1. Line 188).

Quotations from prose works should provide a chapter reference and, where appropriate, a page reference.

Bibliographies should list full details of all sources consulted. The way in which they are presented varies, but one standard format is as follows:

1 Books and articles are listed in alphabetical order by the author's last name. Initials are placed after the surname.
2 If you are referring to a chapter or article within a larger work, you list it by reference to the author of the article or chapter, not the editor (although the editor is also named in the reference).
3 Give (in parentheses) the place and date of publication, e.g. (London, 1962). These details can be found within the book itself. Here are some examples:

> Brockbank, J.P., 'Shakespeare's Histories, English and Roman', in Ricks, C. (ed.) English Drama to 1710 (Sphere History of Literature in the English Language) (London, 1971).
> Gurr, A., 'Richard III and the Democratic Process', Essays in Criticism 24 (1974), pp. 39–47.
> Spivack, B., Shakespeare and the Allegory of Evil (New York, 1958).

Footnotes: In general, try to avoid using footnotes and build your references into the body of the essay wherever possible. When you do use them give the full bibliographic reference to a work in the first instance and then use a short title: e.g. See K. Smidt, <u>Unconformities in Shakespeare's History Plays</u> (London, 1982), pp. 43–47 becomes Smidt (pp. 43–47) thereafter. Do not use terms such as 'ibid.' or 'op. cit.' unless you are absolutely sure of their meaning.

There is a principle behind all this seeming pedantry. The reader ought to be able to find and check your references and quotations as quickly and easily as possible. Give additional information, such as canto or volume number whenever you think it will assist your reader.

SUGGESTIONS FOR FURTHER READING

Bayley, John, *Shakespeare and Tragedy* (London, 1981)

Bradley, A C, *Shakespearean Tragedy* (London, 1904)

Dollimore, Jonathan, *Radical Tragedy: Religion, Ideology and Power in the Drama of Shakespeare and His Contemporaries* (Brighton, 1984)

Empson, William, *The Structure of Complex Words* (London, 1953)

Heilman, Robert B, *Magic in the Web: Action and Language in 'Othello'* (London, 1956)

Holloway, John, *The Story of the Night: Studies in Shakespeare's Major Tragedies* (London, 1961)

Hunter, G K, *Othello and Colour Prejudice* (London, 1968)

Leavis, F R, 'Diabolic Intellect and the Noble Hero', in *The Common Pursuit* (London, 1952)

Muir, Kenneth and Edwards, Philip (eds), *Aspects of Othello* (London, 1977)

Salgado, Gamini and Salgado, Fenella, *Othello: A Critical Study* (Harmondsworth, 1985)

Snyder, Susan, *The Comic Matrix of Shakespeare's Tragedies* (Bloomington, Ind., 1979)

Longman Group UK Limited
Longman House, Burnt Mill, Harlow, Essex, CM20 2JE, England
and Associated Companies throughout the World.

First published 1991
ISBN 0 582 07578 5

*Set in 10/12 pt Century Schoolbook, Linotron 202
Printed in Great Britain by Bell and Bain Ltd., Glasgow*

Acknowledgement
The editors would like to thank Zachary Leader for his assistance with
the style sheet.